Artificial Intelligence and Multimedia Data Engineering

Volume 1

Edited by

Suman Kumar Swarnkar
Shri Shankaracharya Institute of Professional Management and Technology Raipur, Chhattisgarh, India

Sapna Singh Kshatri
Shri Shankaracharya Institute of Professional Management and Technology Raipur, Chhattisgarh, India

Virendra Kumar Swarnkar
Bharti University Durg Chhattisgarh, India

Tien Anh Tran
Vietnam Maritime University Haiphong, Vietnam

Artificial Intelligence and Multimedia Data Engineering

Volume # 1

Editors: Suman Kumar Swarnkar, Sapna Singh Kshatri, Virendra Kumar Swarnkar & Tien Anh Tran

ISBN (Online): 978-981-5196-44-3

ISBN (Print): 978-981-5196-45-0

ISBN (Paperback): 978-981-5196-46-7

First published in 2023.

Bentham Science Publishers Pte. Ltd.
80 Robinson Road #02-00
Singapore 068898
Singapore
Email: subscriptions@benthamscience.net

CONTENTS

PREFACE

Welcome to "Artificial Intelligence and Multimedia Data Engineering Vol. 1". In this book, we embark on a captivating journey through the cutting-edge realms of artificial intelligence (AI) and multimedia data engineering, exploring the remarkable synergies that exist between these two rapidly evolving fields. This fusion of AI and multimedia data engineering has opened up unprecedented opportunities for innovation and has profoundly impacted various industries, making it essential for researchers, practitioners, and enthusiasts alike to stay at the forefront of this dynamic landscape.

Advancements in AI, coupled with the explosive growth of multimedia data, have revolutionized the way we interact with technology and perceive the world around us. From computer vision and natural language processing to deep learning and intelligent systems, AI has become an indispensable part of our lives, shaping our experiences in ways we could have only imagined a few decades ago. Furthermore, multimedia data, including images, videos, audio, and other sensor-generated content, has become an integral part of our digital existence, leading to the creation of a vast ocean of information that needs to be efficiently processed and harnessed.

The primary aim of this book is to present a comprehensive overview of the interdisciplinary domain that intertwines AI and multimedia data engineering. Our endeavor is to provide a well-rounded understanding of the fundamental concepts, techniques, and applications that form the bedrock of this exciting field. Whether you are a seasoned professional seeking to expand your knowledge or a newcomer eager to explore the frontiers of AI and multimedia data engineering, this book caters to a wide audience with diverse interests and backgrounds.

Suman Kumar Swarnkar
Shri Shankaracharya Institute of Professional
Management and Technology
Raipur, Chhattisgarh, India

Sapna Singh Kshatri
Shri Shankaracharya Institute of Professional
Management and Technology
Raipur, Chhattisgarh, India

Virendra Kumar Swarnkar
Bharti University
Durg Chhattisgarh, India

&

Tien Anh Tran
Vietnam Maritime University
Haiphong, Vietnam

List of Contributors

Ankit Kumar	Department of Information Technology, Babu Banarasi Das Institute of Technology, Management, Lucknow, India
Anil Kumar Singh	Department of Information Technology, Babu Banarasi Das Institute of Technology, Management, Lucknow, India
C.A. Harikrishnan	Department of Computer Science and Engineering, Trivandrum, Kerala, India
Darpan Anand	Padampat Singhania University, Udaipur, Udaipur, India
Deepak Asrani	Department of Computer Science and Engineering, BN College of Engineering and Technology, Lucknow, India
Eram Fatima	Department of Information Technology, Babu Banarasi Das Institute of Technology, Management, Lucknow, India
Gausiya Yasmeen	Department of Computer Application, Lucknow, India
Isaac Atta Senior Ampofo	Kwame Nkrumah University of Science and Technology, Kumasi, Ghana
Jayashree Padmanabhan	Anna University, Chennai, India
Mohd Faisal	Department of Computer Application, Lucknow, India
P. Devisivasankari	CMR Institute of Technology, Bengaluru, India
R.K. Kapila Vani	Department of Computer Science and Engineering, Sri Venkateswara College of Engineering, , Valarpuram, Tamil Nadu, India
R. Vijayakumar	CMR Institute of Technology, Bengaluru, India
Richard Essah	Department of Computer Science and Engineering, Chandigarh University, Chandigarh, India
Ritesh Diwaker	Department of Computer Science and Engineering, BN College of Engineering and Technology , Lucknow, India
Saman Uzma	Cubeight Solutions Sydney, Sydney, Australia
Surender Singh	Apex Institute of Technology, Department of Computer Science and Engineering, Chandigarh University, Chandigarh, India
Syed Adnan Afaq	Department of Computer Application, Lucknow, India
Vishal Sharma	Department of Computer Science and Engineering, WILP Faculty, BITS Pilani, Jhunjhunu, Rajasthan, India

CHAPTER 1

A Quantum-assisted Diagnostics Method for Intelligent Manufacturing

Vishal Sharma[1,*]

[1] *Department of Computer Science and Engineering, WILP Faculty, BITS Pilani, Jhunjhunu, Rajasthan, India*

Abstract: Present manufacturing machines have few methods to investigate machine health. To minimize issues and enhance the correctness of machine decisions and automation, machine health conditions require to be investigated. Therefore, the evolution of a fresh investigating and diagnostics approach for additive manufacturing machines is needed for better productivity in Industry 4.0. In the current chapter, an intelligent technique for the condition monitoring of additive manufacturing (AM) is described, where an accelerometer fitted on the extruder assembly is used to receive vibration signals. The process errors with the printer were the worn-out timing belts driving the extruder assembly. Quantum-based Support Vector Machine was simulated to identify the 3D-printer status. The simulation outcomes presented here show that this approach has better correctness as compared to the previous Support Vector Machine techniques.

Keywords: 3D Printer, Additive Manufacturing, Industry 4.0, Support Vector Machine.

INTRODUCTION

3D printer is one of the important fields of research under the Industry 4.0. This technique provides many benefits. Therefore, it is essential to confirm feasible and safety equipment functioning. If mechanical equipment fail, it can create many issues [1 - 3]. Several scientists have done a lot of innovation, and proposed many impactful fault diagnosis approaches [4 - 9]. The recent research work accomplished in the domain of quantum technologies [10 - 19] showed a significant improvement in terms of speed, accuracy, security, and parallel processing with minimum resources.

* **Corresponding author Vishal Sharma:** Department of Computer Science and Engineering, WILP Faculty, BITS Pilani, Jhunjhunu, Rajasthan, India; E-mail: bits.vishal11@gmail.com

Suman Kumar Swarnkar, Sapna Singh Kshatri, Virendra Kumar Swarnkar & Tien Anh Tran (Eds.)

3D printing is a suitable term to detail the techniques of additive manufacturing. The term 3D printing covers many techniques [17]. 3D printing techniques have

the strength to make better science, technology, and engineering as well as to speed up manufacturing techniques. While the possible uses of 3D printing have been enhancing over time, a number of problems continue to stop its widespread acceptance [19]. The main difficulties in 3D printing are increased manufacturing time as compared to standard methods, dimensional correctness, non-linearity (many resolutions for X, Y and Z axes, wall thickness), material properties and system cost. All these are being highlighted by the machine manufacturers for improvement in the manufacturing steps [20].

Even though additive manufacturing has been present since the 1980s, it was not until recently that 3D printing was deployed in commercial manufacturing [19]. Hence, a diagnostics model could be framed for a 3D printer in case of unsuccessful timing belts. Acoustic emissions of 3D printers were also analysed [17, 19]. The printer was run at many nozzle temperatures. The experiments were carried out to analyse the condition monitoring of the nozzle through the deployment of a vibration sensor [21].

Here we try to construct a real-time diagnostic approach for condition monitoring of the machine, in order to find out and preclude breakdowns and process failures. The comprehensive target is to get better process reliability, dimensional correctness of the product, and automation of Additive manufacturing. Mainly, the concentration is on the health status of the belts driving the extruder. They are important parts of a 3D printer device which impact the overall feature and efficiency of the product. In the current chapter, an analysis of the reliability of PHM-based vibration signal analysis is described and based on the results from the signal, a diagnosis model for a 3D printer fault detection is constructed [22].

METHODOLOGY

With the demand of AM, its health status observation has become an important and untouched field of research [23]. The complete working procedure is shown in Fig. (**1**).

Feature Selection

It is required to know important parameters and remove repeated ones.

Fig. (**1**) likely illustrates the steps or stages involved in diagnosing issues or problems related to a 3D printer. It visually represents the diagnostic workflow, showing the sequential or parallel steps involved in identifying and resolving printer malfunctions or errors.

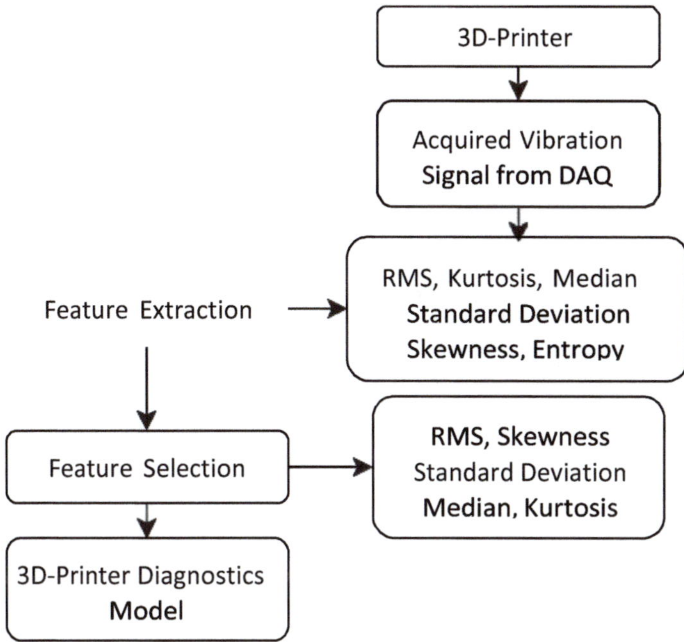

Fig. (1). 3D Printer Diagnostic Process [2].

Results

In Fig. (**2**), 3D-Printer Test Rig likely refers to a figure depicting a test setup or apparatus specifically designed for testing and evaluating 3D printers.

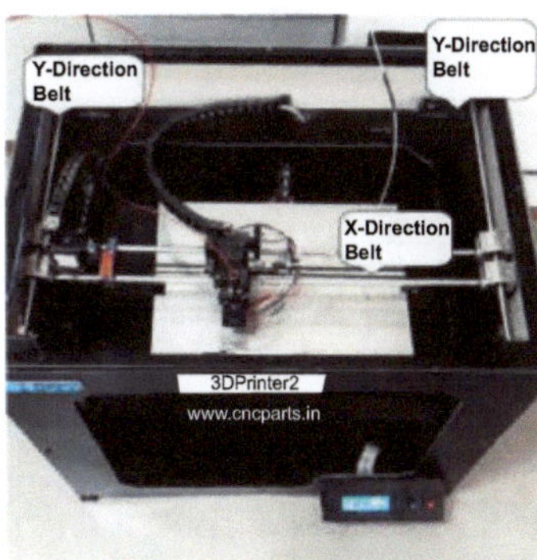

Fig. (2). 3D-Printer Test Rig [2].

Typically, a 3D-Printer Test Rig is a controlled environment that allows researchers or technicians to assess various aspects of 3D printers, such as their performance, accuracy, reliability, and functionality. The test rig is designed to simulate real-world conditions and scenarios to ensure consistent and standardized testing.

Fig. (**2**) illustrates the physical structure of the test rig, including its components and subsystems. It includes a 3D printer, sensors for measuring different parameters, data acquisition systems, control mechanisms, and other relevant equipment.

The purpose of a 3D-Printer Test Rig is to provide a controlled and reproducible environment for evaluating the performance and capabilities of 3D printers. It allows researchers, manufacturers, or quality control personnel to conduct systematic tests, identify potential issues or limitations, and make improvements to enhance the overall quality and efficiency of 3D printing processes [23].

Table **1** provides the values of different condition indicators and their corresponding scores obtained through two evaluation techniques: Univariate Selection and Feature Importance. The indicators listed in the table include Kurtosis, RMS (Root Mean Square), Skewness, Median, Standard Deviation, and Entropy. Each indicator is associated with a numerical value, representing its strength or importance in the given context. The scores provided for Univariate Selection and Feature Importance indicate the relative significance of each indicator for the task at hand [24].

Table 1. Values of condition indicator.

Feature	Univariate Selection	Feature Importance
Kurtosis	146.44	0.166
RMS	99.44	0.2685
Skewness	78.8	0.171
Median	41.24	0.2768
Standard Deviation	14.27	0.1174
Entropy	0.00	0.1053

Table **2** presents various approaches or algorithms' correctness or accuracy rates in different scenarios. The table shows the performance of three algorithms: Random Forest, SVC (Support Vector Classifier), and ANN (Artificial Neural Network). The correctness rates are reported for different comparisons: Fresh *vs.*

Train-Set, Fresh *vs.* Test-Set, and specific belt comparisons (*e.g.*, All Belts, Both Y-Belts, X Belt, *etc.*).

Table 2. Correctness of various approaches.

Algorithms	Random Forest		SVC		ANN	
Fresh v/s	Train-Set	Test-Set	Train-Set	Test-Set	Train-Set	Test-Set
All Belts	100%	100%	98.35%	98.88%	98.35%	98.51%
Both Y-Belts	100%	98.76%	99.18%	98.76%	98.57%	99.59%
X Belt	100%	97.9%	97.93%	97.9%	97.76%	96.86%
X and Y-Belts	100%	94.11%	95.63%	94.48%	91.45%	88.6%
One Y-Belt	100%	99.59%	99.19%	99.59%	98.6%	98.37%
Multi-Class	100%	85.51%	77.03%	82.55%	72.43%	74.45%

For each comparison, the table displays the correctness rates achieved by each algorithm. The percentages provided indicate the corresponding algorithm's accuracy in correctly classifying the data. For example, if an algorithm achieves 100% correctness, it accurately classifies all the instances or samples in the given scenario.

Overall, Table **2** compares the performance of different algorithms across various scenarios, demonstrating their effectiveness in correctly classifying the data based on other criteria [25].

The experimental process for 3D Printer Diagnosis likely illustrates the experimental process or workflow undertaken for diagnosing issues or problems in a 3D printer. It is easier to explain the figure precisely with specific details about the content of Fig. (**3**). However, the figure could include a graphical representation or diagram outlining the steps involved in the experimental process for diagnosing 3D printer issues.

The experimental process involves various stages, such as data collection, measurement, analysis, and testing. It includes preparing the 3D printer, identifying the specific issue or malfunction, conducting tests or experiments, gathering relevant data, analyzing the results, and ultimately diagnosing the problem [26].

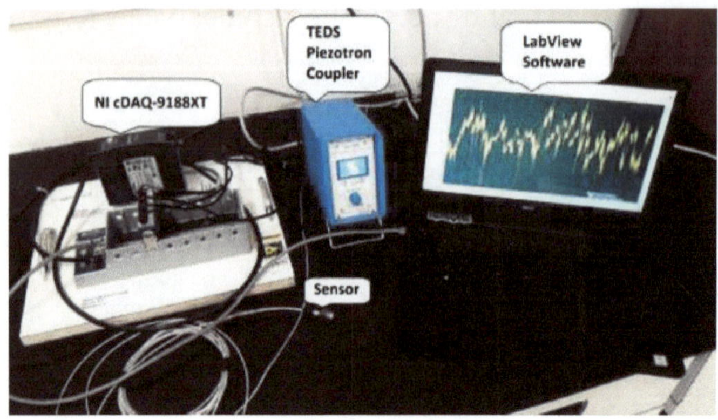

Fig. (3). Considered experimental process for 3D printer diagnosis [2].

Additionally, Fig. (**4**) depicts the equipment, tools, or techniques utilized during the experimental process. It highlights the different components involved, the connections or interactions between them, and the flow of the diagnostic process.

Fig. (4). Sensor deployed to receive vibration signals [2].

CONCLUSION

Loosening and damage of belts are some of the processing errors in AM which impact the correctness of the prototype. In this chapter, a novel approach to the application of an accelerometer to describe this process error is highlighted. Normal and aberrant conditions were detected. The necessary features were detected, which were used in Random Forest, SVM, and ANN classifier. The practical outcomes recommend that vibration sensors validate authenticity for condition monitoring of 3D printers.

Further tests are required to increase the correctness of the multi-class classifier. Mounting of the sensor is very significant to receive correct readings from the data acquisition system. So, RNN models can be developed to speed up the power of the diagnostic system.

REFERENCES

[1] J. Xiong, Q. Zhang, Z. Peng, G. Sun, W. Xu, and Q. Wang, "A diagnosis method for rotation machinery faults based on dimensionless indexes combined with-nearest neighbor algorithm", *Mathematical Problems in Engineering, Hindawi,* 2015.

[2] Q.H. Zhang, "Fault diagnosis in unit based on artificial immune detectors system", *China Petrochemical Press,* 2008.

[3] V. Sharma, and S. Banerjee, "Quantum communication using code division multiple access network", *Opt. Quantum Electron.,* vol. 52, no. 8, p. 381, 2020. [http://dx.doi.org/10.1007/s11082-020-02494-3]

[4] G. Qiu, X. Tang, L. Zhuang, and Z. Yang, "Application of neural network trained by chaos particle swarm optimization to fault diagnosis for rotating machinery", *Zhongguo Jixie Gongcheng,* vol. 19, no. 21, pp. 2642-2645, 2008.

[5] D.Y. Dou, and Y.K. Zhao, "A priority and diagnosis tree-based expert system for fault diagnosis of rotating machinery", *Zhongguo Dianji Gongcheng Xuebao,* vol. 28, no. 32, pp. 82-89, 2008.

[6] V. Sharma, and R. Sharma, "Analysis of spread spectrum in MATLAB", *Int. J. Sci. Eng. Res.,* vol. 5, no. 1, pp. 1899-1902, 2014.

[7] Vishal Sharma, "Effect of noise on practical quantum communication systems", *Defence Science Journal,* vol. 66, no. 2, 2016.

[8] V. Sharma, and A. Bhardwaj, "Analysis of differential phase shift quantum key distribution using single-photon detectors", *2022 International Conference on Numerical Simulation of Optoelectronic Devices (NUSOD)* 12-16 September 2022, Turin, Italy, pp. 17-18, [http://dx.doi.org/10.1109/NUSOD54938.2022.9894772]

[9] J. Xiong, Q. Zhang, G. Sun, X. Zhu, M. Liu, and Z. Li, "An information fusion fault diagnosis method based on dimensionless indicators with static discounting factor and KNN", *IEEE Sens. J.,* vol. 16, no. 7, pp. 2060-2069, 2016. [http://dx.doi.org/10.1109/JSEN.2015.2497545]

[10] V. Sharma, S. Gupta, G. Mehta, and B.K. Lad, "A quantum-based diagnostics approach for additive manufacturing machine, IET Collaborative Intelligent Manufacturing", *Wiley Online Library,* vol. 3, no. 2, pp. 184-192, 2021.

[11] V. Sharma, and S. Banerjee, Analysis of quantum key distribution based satellite communication In 2018 9th International Conference on Com- puting, *Communication and Networking Technologies (ICCCNT),* pp. 1-5, 2018.

[12] V. Sharma, and S. Banerjee, "Analysis of atmospheric effects on satellite-based quantum communication: A comparative study", *Quantum Inform. Process.,* vol. 18, no. 3, p. 67, 2019. [http://dx.doi.org/10.1007/s11128-019-2182-0]

[13] Q Zhang, Y. Qian, and B. Xu, *Control (Chic. Ill),* vol. 28, no. 1, pp. 89-92, 2008.

[14] P. Konar, and P. Chattopadhyay, "Bearing fault detection of induction motor using wavelet and support vector machines (SVMs)", *Appl. Soft Comput.,* vol. 11, no. 6, pp. 4203-4211, 2011. [http://dx.doi.org/10.1016/j.asoc.2011.03.014]

[15] H. Wu, Y. Wang, and Z. Yu, "*In situ* monitoring of FDM machine condition *via* acoustic emission", *International Journal of Advanced Manufacturing Technology, Springer,* vol. 84, no. 5-8, pp. 1483-

1495, 2016.

[16] Jian Zhang, YJ Li, YY Cao, and Lina Zhang, "Immune SVM used in wear fault diagnosis of aircraft engine", *J. Beijing Univ. Aeronaut. Astron,* vol. 43, no. 7, p. 018, 2017.

[17] V. Sharma, C. Shukla, S. Banerjee, and A. Pathak, "Controlled bidirectional remote state preparation in noisy environment: A generalized view", *Quantum Inform. Process.,* vol. 14, no. 9, pp. 3441-3464, 2015.
[http://dx.doi.org/10.1007/s11128-015-1038-5]

[18] J. Yoon, D. He, and B. Van Hecke, "A PHM approach to additive manufacturing equipment health monitoring, fault diagnosis, and quality control", *Proceedings of the Prognostics and Health Management Society Conference,* Fort Worth, TX, USA, Citeseer, 29 (3): pp. 1–9 , 2014.

[19] V. Sharma, K. Thapliyal, A. Pathak, and S. Banerjee, "A comparative study of protocols for secure quantum communication under noisy environment: Single-qubit-based protocols versus entangled-state-based protocols", *Quantum Inform. Process.,* vol. 15, no. 11, pp. 4681-4710, 2016.
[http://dx.doi.org/10.1007/s11128-016-1396-7]

[20] J. O'Callaghan, J. Wells, S. Richardson, H. Holmes, Y. Yu, S. Walker-Samuel, B. Siow, and M.F. Lythgoe, "Is your system calibrated? MRI gradient system calibration for pre-clinical, high-resolution imaging", *PLoS One,* vol. 9, no. 5, p. e96568, 2014.
[http://dx.doi.org/10.1371/journal.pone.0096568] [PMID: 24804737]

[21] ZHANG2019164, "Dynamic condition monitoring for 3D printers by using error fusion of multiple sparse auto-encoder", *Computers in Industry,* vol. 105, pp. 164-176, 2019.
[http://dx.doi.org/10.1016/j.compind.2018.12.004]

[22] V. Sharma, U. Shrikant, R. Srikanth, and S. Banerjee, "Decoherence can help quantum cryptographic security", *Quantum Inform. Process.,* vol. 17, no. 8, p. 207, 2018.
[http://dx.doi.org/10.1007/s11128-018-1974-y]

[23] Y. Tlegenov, G.S. Hong, and W.F. Lu, "Nozzle condition monitoring in 3D printing", *Robot. Comput.-Integr. Manuf.,* vol. 54, pp. 45-55, 2018.
[http://dx.doi.org/10.1016/j.rcim.2018.05.010]

[24] V. Sharma, *Quantum Communication Under Noisy Environment: From The- ory to Applications.* Indian Institute of Technology Jodhpur, 2018.

[25] Y. Tlegenov, Y.S. Wong, and G.S. Hong, "A dynamic model for nozzle clog monitoring in fused deposition modelling", *Rapid Prototyping J.,* vol. 23, no. 2, pp. 391-400, 2017.
[http://dx.doi.org/10.1108/RPJ-04-2016-0054]

[26] I. Campbell, D. Bourell, and I. Gibson, "Additive manufacturing: Rapid prototyping comes of age, Rapid prototyping journal", *Emerald Group Publishing Limited,* vol. 18, no. 4, pp. 255-258, 2012.

CHAPTER 2

Evaluation of Bio-inspired Computational Methods for Measuring Cognitive Workload

R. K. Kapila Vani[1,*] and **Jayashree Padmanabhan**[2]

[1] *Department of Computer Science and Engineering, Sri Venkateswara College of Engineering, Valarpuram, Tamil Nadu, India*

[2] *Anna University, Chennai, India*

Abstract: Evaluating mental workload is crucial to preserve health and prevent mishaps. The reliability and mental states of individuals in any human-computer interaction scenario are assessed utilizing features of the electroencephalogram (EEG) by means of many approaches in machine learning and deep learning This study reviews and identifies the multiple Machine Learning and Deep Learning algorithms used for workload assessment, as well as the various datasets, characteristics, and features that contribute to workload assessment. When ML and DL approaches were compared, it was found that deep learning techniques and ensemble techniques work best when EEG's Power Spectral Density Features are used. We have also used optimization techniques like GWO and taken into account numerous features from various domains and assessed the workload. This study discovered that when measuring cognitive load, features like PSD were employed and deep learning algorithms were applied if algorithm performance was crucial. However, when accuracy was valued more highly, all features were taken into account and only a small subset of them was chosen using optimization techniques. The latter method was found to be more accurate and reliable than the methods currently in use.

Keywords: Cognitive workload, Deep learning, Electroencephalogram (EEG), Machine learning, Optimization techniques.

INTRODUCTION

The Brain Computer Interface (BCI), a key method of communication, enables people to control portable gadgets with their thoughts. The electroencephalogram (EEG) signal is currently the foremost used signal in BCI systems because of its high temporal resolution and utility. It is regarded as an example of non-invasive measurements. Berger was the first person to identify electroencephalography

* **Corresponding author R. K. Kapila:** Department of Computer Science and Engineering, Sri Venkateswara College of Engineering, Valarpuram, Tamil Nadu, India; E-mail: rkkapilavani@svce.ac.in

Suman Kumar Swarnkar, Sapna Singh Kshatri, Virendra Kumar Swarnkar & Tien Anh Tran (Eds.)

(EEG) impulses in the human brain in 1929 and since then more study has been done on brain electrical signals. Research on BCI technology has become a rising trend in recent years, thanks to faster computer hardware, machine learning, and the application of neuroscience [1]. Applications for BCI include disease detection, emotion detection, motion recognition, and e-learning. This study aims to evaluate the effectiveness of several algorithms while assessing the cognitive load or working memory of an individual.

Working memory relates to the capability of tracking numerous bits of knowledge while tackling a single challenge [2]. Cognitive load refers to the task strain placed on working memory, when participating in mental activity [3]. The level of cognitive load that BCI interface users endure is primarily related to how successfully they do their tasks [4]. Cognitive stress is related to working memory tasks requiring executive control. Maintaining the optimal level of cognitive load will increase precision and efficacy. Deteriorating performance in areas like Public transit systems, airline traffic control or combat activities could result in catastrophic accidents [5]. In these industries, the creation and assessment of a job activity necessitate an evaluation of the cognitive strain [6].

Subjective and objective indicators of cognitive workload have been identified and discussed below. Subjective assessments are based on operators' perceptions and self-rating. Cognitive workload is measured by surveys like the National Aeronautics and Space Administration-Task Load Index [7]. Although these methods are easy to use, they do not result in timely and reliable data. However, realistic assessments that focus more emphasis on task performance and physiological indications may be useful in resolving the aforementioned issues [8].

Amongst participants, EEG signals are weak, chaotic, and non-stationary. In light of this, finding significant characteristics in EEG remain a difficulty. Conventional analytical techniques rely on empirical tests to confirm differences between attributes, like power changes with specialized frequency ranges that may not provide sufficient modelling power. The literature has produced a variety of machine-learning techniques to deal with these problems [9]. From data that faithfully reflects the intrinsic rules, machine learning may extract prejudiced traits and utilize them to build prediction models.

Even though numerous papers discuss how to evaluate cognitive workload using a variety of physiological data, many are not aware of the use of machine learning techniques for accurately identifying cognitive burden based on EEG. For instance, a study [10] examines 24 cognitive workload assessment systems that incorporate a wide range of physiological factors. Recent assessments and multimodal integration for the cognitive load put a special emphasis on a number of physiological markers. The objective of this research was to fill the vacuum by reviewing the machine learning and deep learning-based cognitive workload assessment methods and highlighting the most important developments in their application to the identification of cognitive burden [11].

In this study, we assess the cognitive strain with EEG data using different ML and DL techniques. The ideas, applications, and key concepts of cognitive load and machine learning are covered in the subsequent sections. The first section introduces concepts related to cognitive workload [12].

COGNITIVE WORKLOAD

Definition and Applications

The cognitive load is described as "the relationship between the function linking the mental resources requested by a task and those resources accessible to be supplied by the human". Social and contextual influences, individual differences, shifts in functional state, task difficulty, and more can all have an impact on cognitive load [13]. Operators may come across underload, normal, and overload workload conditions in real-world scenarios. Maintaining a healthy and balanced workload can help operators perform safely and productively. In recent years, computer-assisted diagnoses such as cancer, depression, schizophrenia, and autistic spectrum disorder have also used cognitive workload [14].

Task Models

To perceive different cognitive workload states, people are usually needed to engage in tasks of varying complexity levels. The most common technique for simulating cognitive burden is operating a machine in a real or virtual environment or conducting a cognitive task in a controlled laboratory setting. The models are divided into two categories: cognitive and operational [15].

Cognitive Task Model

The participants were generally expected to perform a few physical operations while engaging in mental activity. Reading and mental arithmetic tasks often demand the temporary processing and storage of informative elements. These tasks include the Sternberg working memory test, the n-back working memory test, and others [16].

The n-back task requires the participant to keep track of n different items while deciding if the current stimulus, which could be text or diagrams, matches a sensory input that was shown in n prior trials. The number n determines the degree of difficulty, with one denoting a low level and three denoting a high level. The research shows that accuracy drops as reaction time increases as n grows. In the Sternberg working memory test, participants must recall a range of stimulus groups, hold onto them for a brief period of time [17], and then decide if the presented stimulus has previously been in the memorization categories.

The participants must keep track of the outcomes of the given calculations and determine whether the given value matches the outcomes they calculated previously. The information must be retrieved from a temporal store of prior findings within the mental workspace in order to finish this procedure. Writing frequently employs both addition and subtraction in mathematics. The usage of many numerals and carry numbers can be used to gauge the complexity of an addition assignment [18].

Operational Task Model

The participants in the operational task model carry out a variety of activities. Most often, truckers, air traffic controllers, pilots, and surgeons are tasked to do these types of jobs. In such scenarios, participants are expected to operate the equipment in a real-world or virtual environment [19].

The NASA Multi-Attribute Task Battery (MATB) is a method for assessing the workload and productivity of human operators in non-linear environments [20]. Monitoring, tracking, communication, and light detection are the four subtasks employed in the MATB task. By changing the needs of each subtask, it is possible to build and alter various task difficulty levels. Air traffic controllers commonly manage visual tasks like directing planes on radar with verbal communication with pilots, making managing air traffic a multi-tasking exercise [21]. Traffic management or complexity variations can be used to predict workload.

MACHINE LEARNING

The fastest-growing field in the world today is machine learning, which is a subset of both data science and artificial intelligence. Machine Learning facilitates the development of learning through its experience [22]. The challenge of improving some element of performance when engaged in certain activities through some sort of training is a simple description of machine learning [23].

Machine learning techniques can be categorised into a variety of groups according on the tasks they are used for. These groups include Classification (supervised learning), Clustering (unsupervised learning), Reinforcement learning (semi-supervised learning), Ensemble learning (Bagging and Boosting algorithms), active learning, and transfer learning. The most widely used form of machine learning is supervised learning. When the labeling of all the primary data is known, supervised learning can be used to create a model that can predict outcomes from incoming data [24]. Classification and regression approaches, such as knn (K nearest neighbour), Svm (support vector machine) and LDA (linear discriminative analysis) are commonly used in supervised learning tasks. Numerous studies have shown that machine learning is able to obtain significant information from EEG data [25].

Traditional Machine Learning Techniques to Detect Cognitive Workload

In order to determine the cognitive stress based on EEG, we first briefly describe the basic steps of the machine learning approaches used. The most popular methods for assessing cognitive effort include data preparation, EEG feature extraction, EEG feature selection, wrapping, and embedded approaches, as well as support vector machine classification techniques. Deep learning techniques include Convolution Neural Networks, Recurrent Neural Networks, and Deep Belief Networks as examples of how features can be automatically learned. Deep learning techniques may not require data preprocessing because they can input raw data. In this field, deep learning methods frequently employ calculated features to teach themselves about temporal, spectral, and geographical data [26].

The subsequent subsections provide a description of the key phases in traditional machine learning for workload detection.

Datasets

Here is a collection of EEG datasets that are freely accessible and can be used to measure cognitive effort.

EEGLearn

A public dataset is used comprised of 15 people (eventually 13, after excluding two owing to noise, aged 24 to 33 years). EEG signals are recorded with the help of 64 electrodes and conventional 10-10 placement while performing a Sternberg working memory test with English characters. Following the collection of all 2670 trails, they were divided into 4 workload groups where each corresponds to the size of the memory letters two, four, six, and eight. The workload is increased in proportion to size. For the SIMKAP job, there are three levels of difficulty:

moderate, high, and extremely high; for the resting state, there are two levels of difficulty: low and high [27].

EEGMAT

An EEG dataset from the National Technical University of Ukraine was made available to the public. It included 66 (then 36) undergraduate students between the ages of 18 and 26 who were implanted with 23 EEG electrodes over their scalps in a 10-20 scheme and asked to execute a mental arithmetic task (serial subtraction). Before engaging in a 4-minute mental arithmetic task, participants underwent an EEG recording in a resting state for three minutes. The dataset includes EEG recordings from both the relaxed condition with eyes closed and from the first minute of workload. The subjects were split into excellent scorers and poor scorers based on how well they performed at work. Such a dataset can be used to study cognitive traits as well as brain processes.

Hybrid EEG-NIRS

Twenty-six individuals, ages 17 to 33, completed three cognitive tasks while having their EEG and near-infrared reflectance spectroscopy (NIRS) recordings made. The tasks included the n-back task, the discrimination/selection response task, and the task requiring word creation. The dataset can be utilized for activities including feature extraction, signal task or cross-task analysis, single EEG or NIRS evaluation, signal processing and feature extraction, and hybrid brain-computer interface research. This dataset can also be utilised for other purposes.

WM-EEG

In order to track brain activity for the localization of epileptic episodes, an EEG dataset was gathered from nine patients with epilepsy as they performed a verbal Sternberg working memory test. This dataset allows researchers to explore working memory using difficult-to-find human electrophysiological recordings. It also allows them to perform brain connection analyses.

STEW

The single-session simultaneous capacity (SIMKAP) test, administered to 48 male college students who had 14 electrodes implanted across their heads in a 10-20 pattern, produced an EEG dataset for multi-task cognitive demanding activities. Participants in the SIMKAP multitasking test must check off identical items by contrasting two different panels while responding to aural questions involving arithmetics, comparison, or data lookup.

All tests were carried out on healthy young people, with the exception of the WM-EEG. EEGMAT also receives preprocessed data as opposed to the other three, which receive raw data. Data with extracted attributes and good preprocessing is provided to EEGLearn. It is important to note that a comparison of the results of studies utilizing different datasets is not possible because the tasks and preparation techniques may differ. Studies that compare the same datasets using different methodologies, on the other hand, provide a more meaningful comparison. As a result, data sharing is essential in enhancing model performance [28].

DATA PREPROCESSING

EEG signals are unreliable at representing brain impulses because of their noise and various artefacts that are introduced during the data collection procedure. The collected EEG data must be cleaned up using data preparation and noise removal techniques to reduce the impact of artefacts. As EEG processing technology has advanced, some practical EEG signal visualisation and processing toolboxes, like EEGLAB and MNE-Python, have been introduced in the literature.

a) Data filtering: It is first advised that sufficient filtering be used to remove different types of noises, both very high and low. Band-pass and notch filters are used to filter EEG signals at specific frequencies (e.g., 0.5 Hz to 50 Hz).

b) Re-referencing: Noise in the scalp is produced by a linear change in EEG signals that originates in the reference electrodes. The electrodes' common average or a single channel, such as the mastoid [16] or central electrode CZ, can be used to re-reference the EEG data.

c) Subsampling: For instance, downsampling reduces the data rate from 1000Hz to 256Hz, enabling a faster calculation.

d) Extraction of the epoch: We can separate epochs that are particular to the events to help with the investigation of task-related alterations in EEG.

e) Elimination of Poor channels: It is necessary to eliminate or replace subpar channels with nearby, better channels when they continuously fail to provide information on how the brain works.

f) Artifact removal: There are two methods for getting rid of artefacts: rejection and rectification. Artefact correction entails evaluating the impact of these artefacts on the EEG for tiny and continuous artefacts, such as electrocardiograms, and removing big and transitory artefacts, such as blinks, by rejecting the contaminated EEG epochs.

FEATURE EXTRACTION

Now we have relatively clean data after the data preprocessing. The procedure of extracting the key characteristics of various levels of cognitive strain from EEG is discussed in the section that follows. Cognitive load is now characterized according to time domain, frequency domain, spatial domain, functional connectivity network components, linear dynamics, and nonlinear dynamics.

Time Domain

The most prevalent temporal domain components include event-related potentials (ERP), statistic properties including mean, standard deviation, variance, kurtosis, and skewness, and the Hjorth parameter. EEG characteristics are averaged over time and time-locked to certain stimuli.

Frequency Domain

The frequency information of the EEG is suggested to be displayed using frequency domain analysis. We may divide the frequency band into many sub-bands that are strongly related to human cerebral activity, such as the alpha (8-13 Hz), beta (13-30 Hz), theta (4-8 Hz), delta (0.1-4 Hz), and gamma band (30-80 Hz). Deep sleep, tiredness, engagement, relaxation, alertness, and activity are all related to different levels of the alpha, beta, gamma, theta, and delta bands. Examples of such decomposition methods include those based on the Fourier transform [29].

Spatial Domain

In general, the frontal, parietal, occipital, temporal cortex, and central areas can be distinguished using EEG electrode placements. The frontal and parietal regions are responsive to alterations in workload, according to a previous study. As a result, multiple research leverages the connected channels in diverse fields to directly analyse workload [30]. We can also utilise methods like PCA (principal component analysis), CSP (common spatial patterns), and CCA to extract geographic data (canonical correlation analysis).

Linear Domain

The autoregressive (AR) model has been widely utilised for processing EEG information. The outcome of an event is predicted using data from the present and one or more variables from the past using a linear regression model used for time series analysis [31].

Nonlinear Dynamics

The EEG signals are non-stationary and nonlinear. Nonstationarity describes how the frequency band components of the brain oscillation change in amplitude or shape with time, while nonlinearity describes how the frequency band components are not combined in a linear manner [32]. The irregular and nonlinear components of EEG are described using nonlinear dynamic characteristics. The nonlinear elements of complexity and entropy are the most often employed nonlinear features in workload assessment. Lempel-Ziv examination of complexity and its derivatives largely represent the level of randomness in time series. Another measure that is employed is approximate entropy, which bases future signal amplitude values on knowledge of past amplitude values.

Functional Connectivity Features

To assess the connectivity between different EEG electrodes or brain regions, researchers also use graph theory and functional connectivity network modelling in addition to the aforementioned characteristics. To build functional connectivity networks related to EEG, some techniques can be applied, including partial directed coherence, the partial directed coherence index, and Pearson's correlation coefficient [33].

FEATURE SELECTION

A feature selection step is typically carried out after the feature extraction stage to choose or create a collection of feature sets from EEG data. The learning model's training time is cut down at this phase, and redundant and irrelevant features are eliminated [34], which enhances prediction and population generalisation performance. Additionally, supervised feature selection strategies can be broken down into the filter, wrapper, embedding techniques ensemble, and optimization algorithms.

Filtering Methods

Prior to classification or regression, feature choices are implemented using two procedures in filter techniques. To begin, group-level differences can be discovered and ranked using basic statistical measures such as mean, variance, *etc*. The second phase involves choosing the features with the best scores. As a result, the chosen attributes are input into classifiers [35]. Examples of traditional filter techniques are Fisher score, T-tests, analysis of variance (ANOVA), Relief, minimal-Redundancy-Maximal-Relevance (mRMR), and mutual information. Examples of traditional filter techniques include (ANOVA), Relief, minimal-Redundancy-Maximal-Relevance (mRMR), Fisher score, and mutual information. While the ANOVA can select features from several groups, the t-test, for instance, can only identify differences between two groups. These techniques are straightforward to use and computationally effective, although they could produce a redundant feature set [36]. The two approaches that come after are more intricate and take into account correlations between many features. The relief technique can be used to assess the importance of traits based on their capacity to distinguish between neighbourhood samples; the more significant a feature is, the closer the samples within a class should be. An established filtering method called mRMR looks for features with the highest pairwise and individual relevance to the target class.

Wrapper Techniques

The machine learning model's objective function is maximised or minimised in wrapper techniques before analysing various feature subsets. Forward feature selection and recursive feature elimination are two similar techniques. The RFE technique subtracts one feature from the feature set and uses the remaining features to compute the performance of the model that has been trained and evaluated. The feature that was removed and matched with the best performance was deemed to be the set's lowest contributor and was thus eliminated [37]. In a study on cognitive effort, the grading of qualities was successfully accomplished using an ANN and RFE-like feature analysis. In a cross-task cognitive stress study, RFE also helps in assessing and recognising robust features in the feature set of frequency band characteristics. This study demonstrates that when compared to using all features, feature selection using RFE can improve model generalisation across tasks [38].

Embedded Techniques

Embedded techniques limit the set of key attributes that are chosen as a component of the machine learning process by imposing specific penalties on the machine learning model. Elastic net techniques, which have the lowest absolute shrinkage and selection operator, have the advantages of shorter training time and a good ability to identify correlations between workload labels and features [39].

Ensemble Feature Selection Techniques

Ensemble feature selection framework involves aggregating the results of n-Feature Selection methods into a single subset of relevant characteristics; in which, a single method representing each FS method is used to choose a subset of relevant features. Pooling helps us to derive the final list of features. Pooling is the process of aggregating all subsets of relevant characteristics, where relevant features are the outcomes of single techniques.

Optimization Techniques

Optimization methods like Particle Swarm Optimization (PSO) and Grey Wolf Optimization can be used to extract the best characteristics from the EEG signals in the temporal domain. The general steps of the optimization algorithm are as follows: Initial population, fitness function computation, upgrading of each particle's personal and global bests, modification of the particle's velocity and position, and ending the algorithm based on a stopping condition [40].

In conclusion, statistical characteristics are used to design filter techniques very quickly and easily, but they do not take the learning model into consideration. Wrapper strategies employ the learning model to choose the features, but because they require more computation and training time than the other two types, there may be issues with overfitting. The embedded strategies save training time by combining feature selection and classification, whereas the penalised approaches include more parameters than the other two. The use of filter and wrapper approaches is another popular feature selection technique for workload recognition.

CLASSIFICATION

Machine learning classification algorithms seek to establish a method for categorizing samples into various groups based on the labelled dataset matching their cognitive workload levels. Some of the widely used classifier techniques are discussed below.

SVM builds a hyperplane to find the best decision boundary. The introduction of a kernel function, which converts nonlinear feature space into linear feature space, is the main novelty of SVM. The kernels could be Gaussian radial basis functions, polynomial, or linear. In workload analysis, the kernels of the linear and radial basis functions are frequently used.

A high level of generalisation is maintained while training time is improved with the least-square SVM. The accuracy of a bounded SVM is comparable to that of a regular SVM when conditioned on a single objective function. The issue of overfitting is greatly reduced by the use of three separate multi-kernel SVMs in the ensemble SVM classifier [41].

For tasks requiring verbal and spatial working memory, 8 participants' EEGs collected across 27 channels were used. In order to distinguish between three different levels of difficulty, Gevins *et al.* trained an ANN. The accuracy rates for the four circumstances ranged between 80% and 98% subject-dependent, 83% cross-subject, and 95% confidence cross-session. In a real-time driving activity, the effort levels are classified by employing a linear LDA. This study shows that subjects perform better when exerting less efforts in situations with high workloads. LDA aims to project the input features onto a smaller feature space. It results in well-separated samples from different classes by decreasing the intra-class distance while increasing the inter-class distance. To categorise workload in diverse situations, further versions such as fisher LDA have been used [42].

Deep Learning Models

Unlike the standard mental workload assessment, which normally draws features from the spectral and temporal components, deep learning is able to learn to simultaneously absorb complex multi-domain information. In order to produce accurate EEG models, researchers have started to use deep learning [43].

Deep learning techniques are often used in BCI systems and have lately gained popularity for analysing biomedical signal which is used to monitor human functional condition. Convolution neural network (CNN) is used in a number of studies to evaluate the human condition using EEG, including the identification of emotions and the detection of driver drowsiness [44]. Recurrent neural networks (RNN) and deep belief networks (DBN) are two further deep learning models applied in these fields. The dimensionality of EEG signals should be reduced first before being transformed into new representations with as much information as recommended by deep learning models. A study looks at the uses of several deep learning models (such as RNN and CNN) for interpreting human brain functions and identifying brain disorders using EEG data [45].

PERFORMANCE EVALUATION

Every classifier that is built has its own advantages and disadvantages. Choosing or building relevant models is a difficult task. To find the optimal model for a certain collection of data and tasks, we have included a variety of studies that compare feature extraction and classification techniques in Table **1**. Because of the data-driven features and methodologies, the classifiers are not very consistent and reliable, as we can observe [46]. Last but not the least, SVM with kernel techniques is a simple and reliable way of dealing with nonlinear data, although the modelling capacity may be restricted whenever the dataset size is significant [47]. LDA methods perform badly with tiny and nonlinear data while being quick to compute, inexpensive, and requiring fewer parameters. Shallow neural networks, such as those employed in ANN techniques, may easily handle several classifications which are not possible in SVM and LDA. The five models CNN, RNN, DBN, DAE, and hybrid are listed according to the sequence in which their deep learning models were developed in order to determine cognitive workload. We have found that CNN and hybrid deep models perform the best [48, 49].

Table 1. Cognitive workload detection using various learning models.

S.No	Ref	Dataset	Task	Workload Levels	Feature Domain	Feature Selection	Classifier Models	Accuracy
1.	[14]	Realtime EEG Recordings	Cognitive and Motor Tasks	3	Frequency	Nil	Support Vector Machine	0.75
2.	[27]	Realtime EEG Recordings	Silent Reading	3	Time Time- frequency Spatial	t-Test	Support Vector Machine	0.83
3.	[20]	Realtime EEG Recordings	Working Memory and Complex Tasks	3	Frequency	--	Support Vector Machine	0.82
4.	[26]	Realtime EEG Recordings	Multimedia Learning	4	Non-linear, Functional Connectivity metrics.	Discrete wavelet Transform	Support Vector Machine	0.88
5.	[45]	Realtime EEG Recordings	Multimedia Learning	2	Frequency	MRMR	Support Vector Machine	0.87
6.	[17]	Realtime EEG Recordings	Automation-enhanced cabin air management system(aCAMS)	3	Frequency	RFE	Least square SVM	0.74
7.	[23]	Realtime EEG Recordings	Working Memory	3	Frequency	visual inspection	ANN	0.8
8.	[19]	Realtime EEG Recordings	Arithmetic	7	Time- frequency	Kruskal-Wallis test;	ANN	0.98
9.	[13]	Realtime EEG Recordings	N-Back	3	Frequency	fast Fourier transform	Regularized LDA	0.63
10.	[21]	Realtime EEG Recordings	N-Back	2	Spatial	Mutual Information	Naïve Bayes	0.84

(Table 1) cont.....

S.No	Ref	Dataset	Task	Workload Levels	Feature Domain	Feature Selection	Classifier Models	Accuracy
11.	[22]	Realtime EEG Recordings	multi-attribute task buttery;	3	Time- frequency	fast Fourier transform	Hierachial Bayes	0.80
12.	[46]	Realtime EEG Recordings	Motor tasks	2	Tone(amplitude, Frequency, phase) and level (Peak to peak),statistical analyses (Median,SD,kurtosis, Skewness)	-	Medium ANN	0.998
13.	[28]	Realtime EEG Recordings	Sternberg Task	4	Power map	-	CNN	0.9247
14.	[16]	Realtime EEG Recordings	aCAMS	7	temporal	-	DBN	0.928
15.	[47]	Realtime EEG Recordings	Working Memory	4	ARYule-Walker features	Crow search algorithm	FFNN	0.94
16.	[29]	Realtime EEG Recordings	N-Back, Arithmetic	2	spatial, spectral, temporal		RNN+3DCNN	0.889
17.	[15]	Realtime EEG Recordings	aCAMS	2	Frequency-PSD		Stacked Denoising AutoEncoder	0.74
18.	[24]	STEW	SIMKAP	3	Time Frequency Linear Non Linear	Grey Wolf Optimization	BLSTM-LSTM	0.9280
19.	[43]	STEW	SIMKAP	3	Time Frequency Linear Non Linear	Grey Wolf Optimization	XGBoost	0.9425
20.	[35]	STEW	SIMKAP	3	PSD	Neighborhood Component Analysis	Support Vector Regression (SVR)	0.69

CONCLUSION

In this work, we conduct a thorough assessment of bio-inspired algorithms for cognitive workload detection. We mainly focus on the fundamental procedures of the algorithm including data collection, preprocessing, optimized feature selection, classification, and evaluation. We also examine a number of popular deep learning workload recognition methods. We also go through the main conclusions of this study. Moreover, it has been noted that applying optimization algorithms improves the accuracy and speed of the algorithm. We summarise the unresolved issues and patterns from the dataset in our conclusion, along with the model construction, subject variability, generalizability, and interpretability that still require investigation.

REFERENCES

[1] R. Mehta, and R. Parasuraman, "Neuroergonomics: A review of applications to physical and cognitive work", *Frontiers in Human Neuroscience,* vol. 7, no. 889, 2013.

[2] P. Arico, G. Borghini, G. Di Flumeri, N. Sciaraffa, A. Colosimo, and F. Babiloni, "Passive BCI in operational environments: Insights, recent advances, and future trends", *IEEE Trans. Biomed. Eng.,* vol. 64, no. 7, pp. 1431-1436, 2017. [http://dx.doi.org/10.1109/TBME.2017.2694856] [PMID: 28436837]

[3] X.W. Wang, D. Nie, and B.L. Lu, "Emotional state classification from EEG data using machine learning approach", *Neurocomputing,* vol. 129, pp. 94-106, 2014. [http://dx.doi.org/10.1016/j.neucom.2013.06.046]

[4] J. Heard, C.E. Harriott, and J.A. Adams, "A survey of workload assessment algorithms", *IEEE Trans. Hum. Mach. Syst.,* pp. 1-18, 2018.

[5] S.G. Hart, and L.E. Staveland, "Development of NASA-TLX (Task Load Index): Results of empirical and theoretical research", *Adv. Psychol.,* vol. 52, no. 6, pp. 139-183, 1988. [http://dx.doi.org/10.1016/S0166-4115(08)62386-9]

[6] G.B. Reid, and T.E. Nygren, "The subjective workload assessment technique: A scaling procedure for measuring mental workload", *Adv. Psychol.,* vol. 52, pp. 185-218, 1988. [http://dx.doi.org/10.1016/S0166-4115(08)62387-0]

[7] N. Sciaraffa, P. Aricò, G. Borghini, G.D. Flumeri, A.D. Florio, and F. Babiloni, "On the use of machine learning for EEG-Based workload assessment: Algorithms comparison in a realistic task", *Human Mental Workload: Models and Applications,* pp. 170-185, 2019.

[8] C. R. L., and N. Jim, "Measuring mental workload using physiological measures: A systematic review", *Appl. Ergon.,* vol. 74, pp. 221-232, 2019. [http://dx.doi.org/10.1016/j.apergo.2018.08.028] [PMID: 30487103]

[9] P. Antonenko, F. Paas, R. Grabner, and T. van Gog, "Using electroencephalography to measure cognitive load", *Educ. Psychol. Rev.,* vol. 22, no. 4, pp. 425-438, 2010. [http://dx.doi.org/10.1007/s10648-010-9130-y]

[10] M. Mazher, A. Abd Aziz, A.S. Malik, and H. Ullah Amin, "An EEG-Based cognitive load assessment in multimedia learning using feature extraction and partial directed coherence", *IEEE Access,* vol. 5, pp. 14819-14829, 2017. [http://dx.doi.org/10.1109/ACCESS.2017.2731784]

[11] A. Jimenez-Molina, C. Retamal, and H. Lira, "Using psychophysiological sensors to assess mental workload during web browsing", *Sensors,* vol. 18, no. 2, p. 458, 2018. [http://dx.doi.org/10.3390/s18020458] [PMID: 29401688]

[12] M.A. Almogbel, A.H. Dang, and W. Kameyama, "Cognitive workload detection from raw eeg-signals of vehicle driver using deep learning", *International Conference on Advanced Communication Technology (ICACT),* pp. 1-6, 2018.

[13] C. Tremmel, C. Herff, T. Sato, K. Rechowicz, Y. Yamani, and D.J. Krusienski, "Estimating cognitive workload in an interactive virtual reality environment using EEG", *Front. Hum. Neurosci.,* vol. 13, no. 401, p. 401, 2019. [http://dx.doi.org/10.3389/fnhum.2019.00401] [PMID: 31803035]

[14] W.K.Y. So, S.W.H. Wong, J.N. Mak, R.H.M. Chan, and M. Emmanuel, "An evaluation of mental workload with frontal EEG", *PLoS One,* vol. 12, no. 4, p. e0174949, 2017. [http://dx.doi.org/10.1371/journal.pone.0174949] [PMID: 28414729]

[15] Y. Zhong, and J. Zhang, "Recognition of cognitive task load levels using single channel EEG and stacked denoising autoencoder", *Proceedings of the 35th Chinese Control Conference IEEE* 27-29 July 2016, pp.3907-3912.

[16] Z. Yin, and J. Zhang, "Cross-subject recognition of operator functional states via EEG and switching deep belief networks with adaptive weights", *Neurocomputing,* vol. 260, no. 18, pp. 349-366, 2017. [http://dx.doi.org/10.1016/j.neucom.2017.05.002]

[17] Z. Yin, and J. Zhang, "Operator functional state classification using least-square support vector machine based recursive feature elimination technique", *Comput. Methods Programs Biomed.,* vol. 113, no. 1, pp. 101-115, 2014. [http://dx.doi.org/10.1016/j.cmpb.2013.09.007] [PMID: 24138846]

[18] G.F. Wilson, and C.A. Russell, "Operator functional state classification using multiple psychophysiological features in an air traffic control task psychophysiological features in an air traffic control task", *Hum Factors,* vol. 45, no. 3, pp. 381-389, 2003. [http://dx.doi.org/10.1518/hfes.45.3.381.27252]

[19] P. Zarjam, J. Epps, and N.H. Lovell, "Beyond Subjective Self-Rating: EEG signal classification of cognitive workload", *IEEE Trans. Auton. Ment. Dev.,* vol. 7, no. 4, pp. 301-310, 2015. [http://dx.doi.org/10.1109/TAMD.2015.2441960]

[20] F. Barravecchia, M. Bartolomei, and L. Mastrogiacomo, "Redefining Human–Robot Symbiosis: a bio-inspired approach to collaborative assembly", *Int J Adv Manuf Technol.,* vol. 128, pp. 2043-2058, 2023. [http://dx.doi.org/10.1007/s00170-023-11920-1]

[21] M. Arvaneh, A. Umilta, and I.H. Robertson, "Filter bank common spatial patterns in mental workload estimation", *International Conference of the IEEE Engineering in Medicine and Biology Society* 25-29 August 2015, Milan, Italy, pp. 4749-4752. [http://dx.doi.org/10.1109/EMBC.2015.7319455]

[22] Z. Wang, R.M. Hope, Z. Wang, Q. Ji, and W.D. Gray, "Cross-subject workload classification with a hierarchical Bayes model", *Neuroimage,* vol. 59, no. 1, pp. 64-69, 2012. [http://dx.doi.org/10.1016/j.neuroimage.2011.07.094] [PMID: 21867763]

[23] A. Gevins, M.E. Smith, H. Leong, L. McEvoy, S. Whitfield, R. Du, and G. Rush, "Monitoring working memory load during computer-based tasks with EEG pattern recognition methods", *Hum. Factors,* vol. 40, no. 1, pp. 79-91, 1998. [http://dx.doi.org/10.1518/001872098779480578] [PMID: 9579105]

[24] R. Hefron, B. Borghetti, C. Schubert Kabban, J. Christensen, and J. Estepp, "Cross-Participant EEG-Based assessment of cognitive workload using multi-path convolutional recurrent neural networks", *Sensors,* vol. 18, no. 5, p. 1339, 2018. [http://dx.doi.org/10.3390/s18051339] [PMID: 29701668]

[25] S. Kuanar, V. Athitsos, N. Pradhan, A. Mishra, and K.R. Rao, "Cognitive analysis of working memory load from EEG by a deep recurrent neural network", *International Conference on Acoustics, Speech, and Signal Processing* 15-20 April 2018, Calgary, AB, Canada, 2018, pp. 2576-2580. [http://dx.doi.org/10.1109/ICASSP.2018.8462243]

[26] A.K. Singh, S.R. Swain, D. Saxena, and C-N. Lee, "A bio-inspired virtual machine placement toward sustainable cloud resource management", *IEEE Systems Journal,* vol. 17, no. 3, pp. 3894-3905, 2023. [http://dx.doi.org/10.1109/JSYST.2023.3248118]

[27] P. Zarjam, J. Epps, and F. Chen, "Characterizing working memory load using EEG delta activity", *in Proc. 19th Eur. Signal Process. Conf* 29 August 2011 - 02 September 2011, Barcelona, Spain, 2011, pp. 1554-1558.

[28] Z. Jiao, X. Gao, Y. Wang, J. Li, and H. Xu, "Deep convolutional neural networks for mental load classification based on EEG data", *Pattern Recognit.,* vol. 76, pp. 582-595, 2018.

[http://dx.doi.org/10.1016/j.patcog.2017.12.002]

[29] P. Zhang, X. Wang, W. Zhang, and J. Chen, "Learning spatial–spectral–temporal EEG Features With Recurrent 3D convolutional neural networks for cross-task mental workload assessment", *IEEE Trans. Neural Syst. Rehabil. Eng.,* vol. 27, no. 1, pp. 31-42, 2019. [http://dx.doi.org/10.1109/TNSRE.2018.2884641] [PMID: 30507536]

[30] F. Dehais, A. Duprès, S. Blum, N. Drougard, S. Scannella, R. Roy, and F. Lotte, "Monitoring Pilot's mental workload using ERPs and spectral power with a six-dry-electrode eeg system in real flight conditions", *Sensors,* vol. 19, no. 6, p. 1324, 2019. [http://dx.doi.org/10.3390/s19061324] [PMID: 30884825]

[31] P. Aricò, G. Borghini, G. Di Flumeri, A. Colosimo, S. Pozzi, and F. Babiloni, "A passive brain–computer interface application for the mental workload assessment on professional air traffic controllers during realistic air traffic control tasks", *Prog. Brain Res.,* vol. 228, pp. 295-328, 2016. [http://dx.doi.org/10.1016/bs.pbr.2016.04.021] [PMID: 27590973]

[32] A. Abrantes, E. Comitz, P. Mosaly, and L. Mazur, "Classification of EEG features for prediction of working memory load", In: *Adv. Eng. Softw.* Springer International Publishing, 2017, pp. 115-126. [http://dx.doi.org/10.1007/978-3-319-41947-3_12]

[33] D. Das Chakladar, S. Dey, P.P. Roy, and D.P. Dogra, "EEG-based mental workload estimation using deep BLSTM-LSTM network and evolutionary algorithm", *Biomed. Signal Process. Control,* vol. 60, p. 101989, 2020. [http://dx.doi.org/10.1016/j.bspc.2020.101989]

[34] N. Friedman, T. Fekete, K. Gal, and O. Shriki, "EEG-Based prediction of cognitive load in intelligence tests", *Front. Hum. Neurosci.,* vol. 13, p. 191, 2019. [http://dx.doi.org/10.3389/fnhum.2019.00191] [PMID: 31244629]

[35] W. L. Lim, O. Sourina, and L. P. Wang, "STEW: Simultaneous task EEG workload dataset", *IEEE Transactions on Neural Systems and Rehabilitation Engineering,* vol. 26, no. 11, 2018.

[36] A. Gramfort, M. Luessi, E. Larson, D.A. Engemann, D. Strohmeier, C. Brodbeck, R. Goj, M. Jas, T. Brooks, L. Parkkonen, and M. Hämäläinen, "MEG and EEG data analysis with MNE-Python", *Front. Neurosci.,* vol. 7, no. 7, p. 267, 2013. [http://dx.doi.org/10.3389/fnins.2013.00267] [PMID: 24431986]

[37] W. Peng, EEG preprocessing and denoising.*EEG Signal Processing and Feature Extraction.,* L. Hu, Z. Zhang, Eds., Springer Singapore: Singapore, 2019, pp. 71-87. [http://dx.doi.org/10.1007/978-981-13-9113-2_5]

[38] B.S. Cheema, S. Samima, M. Sarma, and D. Samanta, *Mental workload estimation from EEG signals using machine learning algorithms.* Engineering Psychology and Cognitive Ergonomics, 2018, pp. 265-284. [http://dx.doi.org/10.1007/978-3-319-91122-9_23]

[39] Y. Ke, H. Qi, F. He, S. Liu, X. Zhao, P. Zhou, L. Zhang, and D. Ming, "An EEG-based mental workload estimator trained on working memory task can work well under simulated multi-attribute task", *Front. Hum. Neurosci.,* vol. 8, p. 703, 2014. [http://dx.doi.org/10.3389/fnhum.2014.00703] [PMID: 25249967]

[40] J.A. Blanco, M.K. Johnson, K.J. Jaquess, H. Oh, L.C. Lo, R.J. Gentili, and B.D. Hatfield, "Quantifying cognitive workload in simulated flight using passive, dry EEG measurements", *IEEE Trans. Cogn. Dev. Syst.,* vol. 10, no. 2, pp. 373-383, 2018. [http://dx.doi.org/10.1109/TCDS.2016.2628702]

[41] W. Zheng, and B. Lu, "Personalizing EEG-based affective models with transfer learning", *International Joint Conference on Artificial Intelligence,* pp. 2732-2738, 2016.

[42] D Wu, Y Xu, and B L Lu, "Transfer learning for EEG-Based brain-computer interfaces: A review of progress made since", *IEEE Transactions on Cognitive and Developmental Systems,* pp. 1-1, 2020.

[43] R.K. Kapila vani, and Dr Jayashree Padmanaban, "Assessment of mental workload using XGBoost classifier from Optimized EEG features", *Int. J. Eng. Syst. Model. Simul.,* pp. 109-115, 2020.

[44] Z. Gao, X. Wang, Y. Yang, C. Mu, Q. Cai, W. Dang, and S. Zuo, "EEG-Based spatio–temporal convolutional neural network for driver fatigue evaluation", *IEEE Trans. Neural Netw. Learn. Syst.,* vol. 30, no. 9, pp. 2755-2763, 2019. [http://dx.doi.org/10.1109/TNNLS.2018.2886414] [PMID: 30640634]

[45] R Sarailoo, K Latifzadeh, SH Amiri, A Bosaghzadeh, and R Ebrahimpour, "Assessment of instantaneous cognitive load imposed by educational multimedia using electroencephalography signals", *Front. Neurosci.,* vol. 16, p. 744737, 2022. [http://dx.doi.org/10.3389/fnins.2022.744737]

[46] D. Singh, and S. Singh, "Realising transfer learning through convolutional neural network and support vector machine for mental task classification", *Electron. Lett.,* vol. 56, no. 25, pp. 1375-1378, 2020. [http://dx.doi.org/10.1049/el.2020.2632]

[47] F.J. Ramírez-Arias, E.E. García-Guerrero, E. Tlelo-Cuautle, J.M. Colores-Vargas, E. García-Canseco, O.R. López-Bonilla, G.M. Galindo-Aldana, and E. Inzunza-González, "Evaluation of machine learning algorithms for classification of EEG signals", *Technologies,* vol. 10, no. 4, p. 79, 2022. [http://dx.doi.org/10.3390/technologies10040079]

[48] M. Thilagaraj, S. Ramkumar, N. Arunkumar, A. Durgadevi, K. Karthikeyan, S. Hariharasitaraman, M.P. Rajasekaran, and P. Govindan, "Classification of electroencephalogram signal for developing brain-computer interface using bioinspired machine learning approach", *Comput. Intell. Neurosci.,* vol. 2022, pp. 1-17, 2022. [http://dx.doi.org/10.1155/2022/4487254] [PMID: 35251147]

[49] S.S. Kshatri, and D. Singh, "Convolutional neural network in medical image analysis: A review", *Arch. Comput. Methods Eng.,* vol. 30, no. 4, pp. 2793-2810, 2023. [http://dx.doi.org/10.1007/s11831-023-09898-w]

CHAPTER 3

Managing Libraries and Information Centres using Cloud Computing

C. A. Harikrishnan[1,*]

[1] *Department of Computer Science and Engineering, Trivandrum, Kerala, India*

Abstract: Cloud computing is basically a new phenomenon for providing services over the internet. The biggest plus point of cloud computing is that it uses third-party hardware and software applications for providing services. It is very much cost-effective and easy to maintain. This type of emerging technology is being adopted by the 21st century libraries and information centres. Cloud computing can be used in libraries to provide better services. Cloud computing allows users of the library to access information from any geographic location. Cloud computing is helpful for libraries and information centres in automating and managing their services.

Keywords: Automation, Cloud computing, Digital library, OPAC, Repository.

INTRODUCTION

Information and communication technology has made revolutionary changes in the functioning of libraries and information centres [1]. Now we have libraries and information centres without walls. Information can be accessed by the users with the help of Cloud computing services without even visiting libraries or information centres. Libraries are now acting as data centre which require computers to operate in a better way. The latest trend in the field of Library and Information Science is the use of cloud computing for storage and retrieval of information. There is a paradigm shift from traditional library management to a more systematic, technical and user-oriented one. Cloud computing offers more personalized service which ultimately leads to more user satisfaction [2].

Multinational companies like Amazon, Microsoft, Google and so on are developing cloud computing systems and providing services to a wide variety of

* **Corresponding author C.A. Harikrishnan:** Department of Computer Science and Engineering, Trivandrum, Kerala, India; E-mail: drharikrishnanca@gmail.com

Suman Kumar Swarnkar, Sapna Singh Kshatri, Virendra Kumar Swarnkar & Tien Anh Tran (Eds.)

users. There are basically three segments in cloud computing; they are: i) Application, ii) Storage and iii) Connectivity. Each of these segments serves a different purpose and also offers different types of products for business purpose and for individual purposes.

DEFINITION OF CLOUD COMPUTING

The National Institute of Technology and Standards (NIST) defines Cloud computing as a model for enabling, convenient, on-demand network access to a shared pool of configurable computing resources [3].

Garner defines cloud computing as a style of computing where massively scalable IT-related capabilities are provided as a service using Internet technologies to multiple external customers.

CHARACTERISTICS OF CLOUD COMPUTING

i. It supports a wide group of platforms such as workstations and mobile devices.

ii. It works efficiently with multiple users and multiple applications.

iii. It reduces the cost of services.

iv. It works very fast in the distributed computing environment.

v. Users can access information from any corner of the world with the help of network/internet connectivity.

vi. There are very less chances of infrastructure failure. It is reliable and ensures on-demand provision of resources.

vii. Resource usage can be monitored and measured based on utilization by the users.

viii. Cloud computing applications are installed on a common platform and can be accessed from various places.

ix. Services can be accessed using Application Programming Interfaces on the cloud and it can be paid as per the usage.

TYPES OF CLOUD

Public Cloud

A public cloud environment is owned by a cloud provider and is accessible to many businesses through the Internet. Public clouds are ideal for small and medium-sized businesses whose budget is less [4].

Private Cloud

A private cloud is owned by a single business party/firm. It offers a more controlled environment. It can offer a higher level of security and autonomy [5].

Hybrid Cloud

A hybrid cloud model provides a tailored IT solution, seeking the benefit of both public and private cloud models.

SERVICES PROVIDED BY CLOUD COMPUTING

Platform as a Service

It provides customers the freedom to build their own applications which run on the provider's infrastructure. Platform as a service provider offers a predefined combination of OS and application servers such as restricted J2EE, Ruby, *etc.* [6].

Examples: Google's App Engine, Force.com *etc.*

Infrastructure as a Service

It provides basic storage and computing capabilities as standardized services over the network. The customer can typically deploy his own software on the infrastructure.

Example: Amazon, 3 Tera, Go Grid *etc.*

Software as a Service

In this model, the customer needs not to invest in servers and software licences, while for the provider, the cost is lowered because only a single application needs to be hosted and maintained [7].

Examples: Microsoft, Zoho *etc.*

TYPES OF COMPUTING TECHNIQUES

Cluster Computing

It connects different computers in a single location *via* a Local Area Network.

Distributed Computing

It enables peer-to-peer computing. ATMs and intranet are examples of such cloud infrastructure.

Invasive Sensors

Invasive sensors, also known as implantable sensors, are permanently implanted inside the human body. The implantation process of these sensors necessitates a surgical operation. Due to the complexity and precision required, the proper implantation of these sensors calls for the expertise of skilled surgeons [8].

Grid Computing

It enables computing jobs using interconnected computers spread across multiple locations that run independently.

Utility Computing

It laid the foundation of today's cloud computing. It provides services such as storage space, computing and applications to users at low cost.

LATEST INITIATIVES OF CLOUD COMPUTING BY VARIOUS COMPANIES/ORGANIZATIONS

Many Cloud computing services are provided to individuals, business groups and organizations by multinational companies like Amazon, Microsoft, Google *etc*. Some of the initiatives of these companies are mentioned below [9]:

Amazon Web Services

Amazon offers a wide variety of services such as Elastic Compute Cloud, Simple storage service, simple queuing service, *etc*. Amazon Web Services provides an affordable, reliable and scalable platform that helps to run thousands of government, private and public firms/organizations throughout the world [10].

Microsoft Azure

Microsoft Windows Azure offers computing, storage, database management, *etc.* for business groups and various other organizations. Organizations can build and run their own applications. Users have to pay for the services they have chosen. Microsoft Azure gives the freedom to developers to develop and run the application quickly [11].

Google Apps

Google Apps are available free of cost for organizations (limited to up to 10 user accounts), individuals, non-profit organizations, educational institutions, *etc.* For business purposes, payment has to be made. Google app offers many services like Gmail, Google Classroom, Google Docs, Google Videos, *etc.* Gmail is the most commonly used email service. In Covid-19 pandemic situation, the majority of educational institutions have depended on Google Classroom, which was very helpful in the teaching and learning process. Google also provides Google App Engine Service, and with the help of this service, organizations can develop and host web applications on the same systems that power Google applications [12].

NEED FOR CLOUD COMPUTING IN LIBRARIES

Cloud computing can the used in areas where a lot of money is required for the implementation of information communication devices. In Modern libraries, Integrated Library Management Software is used. It provides services like OPAC, an institutional repository, a circulation module, an acquisition module, a serial control module, a reporting module, a library website, and digital library. Installation, configuration and annual maintenance of information communication devices are expensive. These are maintained by the library staff of a particular library or information centre. It is at this juncture the role of cloud computing comes into play [13]. Cloud computing runs different information and communication services. It will manage servers, undertake upgrades and take backups of data. Cloud computing can improve library facilities and services. Cloud computing helps in the sharing of information in a speedy way.

CLOUD COMPUTING SERVICES AND ITS APPLICATIONS IN THE LIBRARY

Information and communication technology plays an important role in handling library resources ranging from collection, storage, organization, and processing to the dissemination of information. Advancements in information and communication technology have created an impact on libraries and information centres also. The latest advancement is towards the formation and maintenance of virtual libraries. Most of the libraries and information centres have online catalogues and they share the data with the Online Computer Library Centre. OCLC uses cloud computing for sharing bibliographic data with libraries and information centres [14].

Library Automation

Polaris software has entered into cloud computing. It provides various cloud-based services such as acquisition, cataloguing, digital content *etc.* for the inclusion of cutting-edge technologies used in libraries for library automation purposes. It supports various standards such as MARC 21, UNICODE, XML, Z39.50 *etc.* [15].

Digital Library and Repository

Most modern libraries and information centres have their own digital libraries. Greenstone, Dspace, Fedora, *etc.* are the most common software tools for building and distributing digital libraries and repositories. Dura Cloud is an open-source technology project which provides complete solutions for developing digital libraries and repositories [15].

Website Hosting

Hosting a website is an adoption of cloud computing. Most libraries and information centres have their own websites. In most of these cases, the websites are maintained by third-party service providers.

Searching Scholarly Content

Libraries and information centres are using various cloud computing platforms for searching and sharing scholarly content. Recently, the Information and Library Network has incorporated the Knimbus Cloud service into its UGC INFONET

DIGITAL Library Consortium. Knimbus is a cloud-based research platform that facilitates sharing and searching scholarly content [16].

Storage and Retrieval of Information

Cloud computing presents a number of services to store and retrieve information. Google Docs, Sky Drive, and Jungle Disk are examples of these types of services. These services share the file on the web and provide access to it anywhere and at any time without the usage of any external hardware.

CLOUD COMPUTING PLATFORMS IN LIBRARY AND INFORMATION SCIENCE FIELD

DuraCloud by Duraspace

DuraCloud helps libraries and information centres to move data to the cloud and store it with different service providers to prevent the risk of data loss.

Webscale by OCLC

OCLC uses Cloud computing for libraries and information centres. The main purpose of using webscale is that libraries can share their data and resources easily.

Ex-Libris Cloud

Ex-Libries is a prominent software vendor from the USA. It provides cloud based solutions to automate the library operations.

OSS Labs

OSS Labs offer hosting and maintenance services for DSpace and Koha. OSS Labs use Amazon's cloud services. Library operations are carried out easily and in a cost-effective manner. The staff of the libraries and information centres need not to worry about the maintenance of the software.

ENHANCING VARIOUS SERVICES PROVIDED BY THE LIBRARIES AND INFORMATION CENTRES USING CLOUD COMPUTING

E-Learning

In the E-Learning environment also, cloud computing is a great boon. Study materials can be kept on the cloud for reference purposes. Online examinations can also be conducted.

File/Document Sharing

Sharing of files, documents, videos, audios *etc.* become easy with the use of cloud computing.

Interaction with the Users

Social interaction with the users can be done with the help of cloud computing.

Fig. (**1**) is a graphical representation or diagram outlining the steps involved in the experimental process for diagnosing 3D printer issues.

The experimental process involves various stages: data collection, measurement, analysis, and testing. It includes preparing the 3D printer, identifying the specific issue or malfunction, conducting tests or experiments, gathering relevant data, analyzing the results, and ultimately diagnosing the problem.

Additionally, the figure might depict the equipment, tools, or techniques utilized during the experimental process. It could highlight the different components involved, the connections or interactions between them, and the flow of the diagnostic process.

Collection Development

Cloud computing helps a lot in data collection in libraries and information centres. Sharing of resources through Cloud computing services helps in the collection process.

Information Search and Discovery

Cloud provides a common platform to store data or information so that one can retrieve information by sitting anywhere in this world. Search and discovery of information is made easy with the help of Cloud Computing.

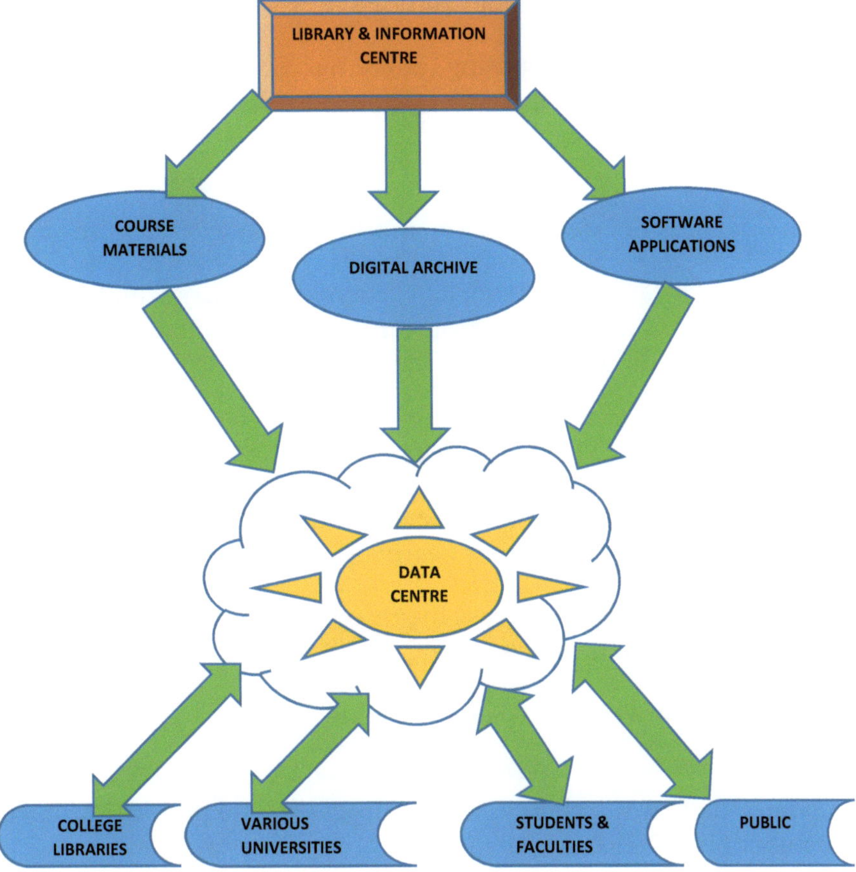

Fig. (1). A model library & information centre working on cloud computing.

Lending of E-books

One of the latest service provided by the cloud platform is that it helps in lending of E-books.

Shared Catalogue/Union Catalogue/OPAC

The libraries which were connected to each other can use the same platform to access their collection. With the help of cloud computing, Union catalogue can be developed very easily.

Document Download and Delivery Service

With the help of Cloud Computing, if the access is allowed/permitted in the network for the library staff, then the documents asked by the users can be easily downloaded and delivered to them.

Current Awareness Service and Information Literacy/Orientation

Providing current awareness service has become very easy with the help of Cloud Computing. Libraries and Information centres can organize information literacy and User orientation programmes on Cloud.

ROLE OF LIBRARIAN IN THE CLOUD ENVIRONMENT

i. The primary role is to communicate with the member libraries to contribute their resources to Cloud for resource sharing.

ii. To provide the users, pin to access the resources. Pin can be auto-generated and the validity can be set in the software.

iii. To communicate with the database providers, e-books, e-Journal publishers and distributors.

iv. To update one's own technological skills and also to provide technical support to the member libraries as and when needed.

v. To conduct orientation programmes/user education programmes for the users of the library and its cloud computing services.

vi. To develop digital collection, (e-books, e-journals *etc.*) consortia and database.

vii. To provide an interlibrary loan facility to the users.

viii. To track the usage record of the cloud resources by the users of the library.

ADVANTAGES OF CLOUD COMPUTING IN LIBRARY SERVICES

Cloud OPAC

Majority of the libraries and information centres maintain their catalogue over the Internet. Catalogues that are made available through cloud are more beneficial to users compared with the old traditional card catalogue system [17].

Less Cost Involved

The use of a hardware and software in some cases can be reduced by the use of cloud computing so that the cost involved in the purchase of hardware and software can be reduced.

Scalability

Pay as and when you use the cloud computing services. It helps in the effective control of expenditure.

Accessibility

We can access information resources by sitting anywhere in the world. Accessibility of data from any geographical point is an added advantage of cloud computing.

Higher Level Security

Cloud computing allows testing and evaluation of resources at no cost. A greater level of security is an advantage of using cloud computing services.

Portability

As the services are provided *via* web, portability has no impact on cloud computing. Information can be accessed by sitting anywhere in the world.

Reduced Risk Rate

The risk rate is very low in using Cloud computing as there is a high level of security in cloud computing and also these are managed by experienced and knowledgeable service providers.

Adjustable Storage

The traditional way is to use server computers in the library which needs constant updation as and when the storage becomes full but if the library is using cloud computing services, then storage capacity can be adjusted according to the needs of the library and information centres. The storage is controlled by the service providers [18, 19].

CONCLUSION

Cloud Computing is a new development in the field of computer systems technology. Cloud computing offers its services over the Internet. Cloud computing is very much needed for managing libraries and information centres in this 21st century. The greatest benefit for libraries and information centres is that it offers services using the hardware and software of third-party sources. It is cost-effective and hassle free as it saves investment cost and the maintenance cost. This technology is very helpful for libraries and information centres in automation and managing the services. By adopting cloud computing in libraries and information centres, the library staff will be free from managing the servers. Technological advancement will flourish in libraries and information centres if Cloud computing services are used in a proper way and with great care.

REFERENCES

[1] Available from: http://en.wikipedia.org/wiki/Cloud_computing

[2] D.A. Kumar, and S. Mandal, "Development of cloud computing in integrated library management and retrieval system", *Int. J. Lib. Inf. Sci.,* vol. 5, no. 10, pp. 410-416, 2013.

[3] S.Y. Bansode, and S.M. Pujar, "Cloud Computing and Libraries", *DESIDOC J. Libr. Inf. Technol.,* vol. 32, no. 6, pp. 506-512, 2012.
[http://dx.doi.org/10.14429/djlit.32.6.2848]

[4] E.S. Mark Shane, "Cloud computing and collaboration", *Library Hi Tech News,* vol. 26, no. 9, pp. 10-13, 2019.

[5] S. Dhamdhere, and R. Lihikar, "Information common and emerging cloud library technologies", *Int. J. Libr. Inf. Sci.,* vol. 5, no. 10, pp. 410-416, 2013.

[6] Available from: http://aws.amazon.com/what-isaws/

[7] S.S. Kshatri, D. Bhonsle, S. Tiwari, R. Mishra, T. Rizvi, and R. Pandey, "Sensor-based devices and their applications in smart healthcare systems", In: *Cognitive Sensors* vol. 1. IOP Publishing, 2022, pp. 2053-2563.
[http://dx.doi.org/10.1088/978-0-7503-5326-7ch9]

[8] Available from: https://developers.google.com/appengine/?csw=1

[9] Available from: http://www.microsoft.com/enterprise/ittrends/cloudcomputing/default.aspx#fbid=gB0X9apRw93

[10] Available from: http://www.rackspace.com/cloud/

[11] R. Fox, "Library in the clouds", *OCLC Syst. Serv.,* vol. 25, no. 3, pp. 156-161, 2009.
[http://dx.doi.org/10.1108/10650750910982539]

[12] Available from: http://www.oclc.org/worldshare-management-services.en.html

[13] Available from: https://exlibrisgroup.com/

[14] Available from: ht tp: //www. exli br isg roup. com/ ?cat id ={BC76 D337 -FEFA -4603 -B827 -

28AB9 F818 - BDB }

[15] Available from: http://www.duracloud.org

[16] Available from: http://www.osslabs.biz/news/oss-labs-host-itssolutionsamazons-cloud-computing-platform

[17] Available from: http://journal.code4lib.org/articles/2510

[18] Available from: http://www.webhostingreport.com/learn/advantages-of-cloud-computing.html

[19] Available from: http://www.informit.com/articles/article.aspx?p=1324280&seqNum=2

CHAPTER 4

Biometric Voting using IoT to Transfer Vote to Centralized System: A Bibliometric

Richard Essah[1,*], **Darpan Anand**[2], **Surender Singh**[3] and **Isaac Atta Senior Ampofo**[4]

[1] *Department of Computer Science and Engineering, Chandigarh University, Chandigarh, India*

[2] *Padampat Singhania University, Udaipur, India*

[3] *Apex Institute of Technology, Department of Computer Science and Engineering, Chandigarh University, Chandigarh, India*

[4] *Kwame Nkrumah University of Science and Technology, Kumasi, Ghana*

Abstract: Several studies have empirically explored biometric voting using the IoT to transfer votes to the central system. There aren't many bibliometric studies that categorize the output in this area, though. By keeping an eye on the papers posted on the Scopus platform, this study's goal is to present a research bibliometric analysis of biometric voting utilizing IoT to transfer votes to a central system, classifying trends, the state of the art, and other indications. 267 different materials made up the sample. Using the VOS viewer program, the data was processed and the outcomes graphically represented. According to a study, that examined publications' simultaneous occurrence by year, trends of keyword, co-citations, coupling bibliographic, and co-authorship analysis, institutions, and countries, the body of knowledge on biometric voting that uses the Internet of Things to transfer votes to a central system is expanding quickly. More than 530 citations were found in just eight works. However, there are other industrious writers. The most significant of the 267 sources used in the review were published in 26.066 percent of the papers. China is the world's leader in this field. This study offers knowledge about the current state of the art and indicates research opportunities and gaps in IoT-based biometric voting.

Keywords: Blockchain, Bibliometric, Centralised system, IoT, Vos viewer.

INTRODUCTION

The astounding spread and quick development of technology in many spheres of life has greatly aided humankind as a whole [1]. Voting has historically been the main way for people to express their thoughts on topics and subjects that are imp-

* **Corresponding author Richard Essah:** Department of Computer Science and Engineering, Chandigarh University, Chandigarh, India; E-mail: Richardeessah84@gmail.com

ortant to them [2]. Voting is a democratic practice. The election process is crucial in democracies because it takes place on a regular basis with the participation of people who have attained voting age and are permitted to do so. Because of this, it is urgently necessary to guarantee the integrity of the elections by providing citizens with protection and security so that they can vote in comfort [3]. Many nations have had authoritarian governments that lacked honesty and openness in the voting process. Having an election system focused on safety, integrity, protecting votes from repetition, manipulation, and tampering, as well as faster results delivery, is a solution for several governments seeking to improve and demonstrate their transparency and credibility in the public eye [4]. In democratic administrations, the practice of voting is utilized to allow the populace to select their representatives. Modern democracies are founded on voting, whether it is by electronic voting (e-voting) or traditional voting based on ballots. Apathy voters have been rising recently, particularly among the younger, more tech-savvy generation [5]. E-voting is promoted as a potential way to get more young people to vote [6, 7]. Many security and functional requirements, such as transparency, correctness, auditability, data and system integrity, privacy and secrecy, authority distribution, and availability, are listed for a reliable e-voting scheme [8 - 10]. Our suggested method depends on blockchain and Internet of Things (IoT) technology to provide security and high performance because the IoT and its applications have become nations' future looking to expand their fields [11]. IoT is viewed as numerous devices' collection linked together in a network to exchange data that, once processed, can be utilized to make the proper decisions when they are needed. The word "IoT" often defines interconnected objects' networks. It is made up of billions of interconnected "things" or gadgets that can perceive, calculate, communicate, and maybe trigger [12]. The technology of blockchain has been around since the 1980s, and today there is more interest in it than ever before thanks to the 2009 invention of the digital currency known as Bitcoin [13]. Blockchain equations were the technology used in the development of Bitcoin, which was regarded as a widely used digital currency in financial transactions. Credibility and security issues affect voters' ability to cast valid ballots in elections. Others stay away from the polls to escape the commotion and lengthy lines. The use of traditional voting procedures in elections has a number of drawbacks, including fraud in the voting process; stuffing extra ballots; faking certain ballots; difficulty with counting; and delays in reporting the results. For governments, the voting process is challenging because of all these issues. To tackle these issues, it is a good idea to create a quick, secure, and dependable system [14]. In some nations, such as India, for example, there is a difficulty with voting centers (kiosks), as they are not widely dispersed. Because these facilities are located in different locations, remote from some communities, they require employees to maintain them. Voters must travel great distances to cast their ballots, which will decrease the number of citizens who should vote. As a result, our method is viewed as a solution to this problem because machines do not require human intervention to operate, allowing authorities to position them near all populous areas and are capable of placing multiple devices in the same space. Voting centers, punch-card voting, optical scan voting, and electronic voting are a few examples of technologies that were deployed (kiosks). It also covers a variety of network types, including mobile networks, private computer networks, and online social media usage. These outdated electronic voting systems have evolved, though, as a result of technical advancements, and the academic community is now more interested than ever in voting equipment that uses the Internet of Things [15]. This system will only be used in government elections. Likewise, in questionnaires and referendums, as well as by private and governmental organizations to learn what the public thinks about a particular service or product, or by community organizations or institutions that want to understand what the general public thinks about a particular issue. The solution depends on blockchain and the IoT working together to provide speed, efficiency, and security in biometric voting. Similar studies have been done on biometric voting using IoT to transfer vote to centralized system [16, 17]. Thus, there is the need to measure these similar studies as well as to assess the productivity of specific scholars, nations, journals, and other performance levels.

LITERATURE REVIEW

Along with the suggested works in this paper to advance the voting electronic process and improve its reliability and efficiency, we will present several solutions that were stated in previous researchers' works that combined electronic voting and blockchain in this section to permit decentralization for the voting electronic process and its services. South Korea participated in tests with electronic voting on the blockchain. Gyeonggi-do Province launched it in March 2018 and did so initially. Officials feel that despite the fact that this was only tried on a small scale, with only 9,000 participants, it demonstrates the possibility of adopting Blockchain technology for voting online [18]. A specific mechanism has been put forth by researchers in an effort to address the issues with the central electronic voting procedure. By fragmenting and encrypting the data and building a network of peer-to-peer, the blockchain technology of Ethereum, which is centered on a network decentralized, assures a secure vote. It is the method of uniquely identifying a vote using the Aadhar number provided by the government, which is connected to a distributed ledger that buries the inner difficulties of the consumer. By connecting all voters with a private and public key, it is possible to assure voter verification and prevent double voting. Because the Aadhar number verification technique is not totally secure, additional measures like a verification code and biometric authentication One Time Password (OTP) must be used. In a different piece, they build and enhance electronic voting while increasing its effectiveness on the blockchain of Ethereum. Through the mobile phone number of the voter, a decentralized and trustworthy approach for guaranteeing data transparency and accuracy has been presented. The voter can then cast his or her ballot using the verification system of the OTP, which transmits a code to the phone number of the voter. So that each vote is associated with just one phone number, increasing the effectiveness of verifying the vote, as they say. However, the necessity for biometric verification is essential and required to dispel any uncertainty regarding confirming that the person actually cast their ballot and not someone else. Another security flaw is the absence of verification using a government-issued voting card number. A plan to create a voting electronic system founded on smart contracts and blockchain that ensures voter security and privacy was put forth in the paper [19]. By connecting a phone number and the Aadhar card, the two methods were also connected to validate the vote before it was cast. The OTP is delivered to the phone of the voter to enable him to cast his vote just once, but there is no method to ensure that the person casting the vote is actually the voter, which is the biggest disadvantage.

REVIEW METHODOLOGY

The bibliometric review of biometric voting using IoT to convey votes to a central system is the basis for this work. The bibliometric review methodology is significant because it offers a classified perspective of the publications in each study field based on impartial standards for evaluating and categorizing publications. In turn, using the VOSviewer software gives the option to exhibit the data graphically using category maps. Data from one of the most significant bibliographic databases, Scopus, was gathered in January 2012. Information was gathered from the Scopus database, which includes additional sub-databases. The query for the terms "internet of things" yielded a total of 137,008 results; "transfer vote" yielded a total of 4 results; and "voting" yielded a total of 55,238. The query for the terms "internet of things, voting, and transfer vote" yielded a total of 267 results. Operators of Boolean were used to filter the outcomes: TITLE-ABS-KEY ("Internet of Things" AND voting OR "transfer vote"). The mechanisms employed to analyze and interpret the data gathered were bibliometric indicators, which were used in the bibliometric analysis [20]. 267 bibliographic resources were collected after the use of Boolean operators; these materials are examined in the current study. A similarity visualization application (VOSviewer) was used to analyse the data and illustrate some of the potential outcomes graphically. The study made use of authorship analysis between both nations and institutions, keyword trends, co-citation, bibliographic coupling, and simultaneous occurrence of publications by year. According to influence, major journals, publications, themes, authors, institutions, and nations, the findings identified the status of development and the key trends. With results relating to biometric voting using IoT to transfer votes to a central system and mapping the key trends in the area, graphic representation, and analysis are crucial because they can aid professionals and academics in understanding what is being researched in the sustainability field. A quotation is created when the same article is quoted in two different documents. The author, journal, and document all use this strategy. The most frequently used terms in papers are measured by the author's co-occurrence of keywords. Once 2 documents cite similar documents, this is known as coupling bibliographic, and co-authorship shows the number of publications for a group of variables and how they are related to one another [21]. It is possible to use this strategy with organizations and nations.

RESULTS AND DISCUSSION

Publications by Year

Studies associated with biometric voting using IoT to transfer votes to a central system started in 2012 with 3 publications. It dropped in 2013 to 2 publications and further dropped in 2014 to 1 publication. The publications started increasing in 2015 and from there, it kept on increasing (Fig. **1**). The last article related to biometric voting using IoT to transfer votes to a central system that was identified in Scopus is from 2022 and it was published in Future Generation Computer Systems with the title "Improving IoT data availability *via* feedback- and voting-based anomaly imputation" by Li *et al.* [22]. This article aimed to "develop a feedback-and voting-based anomaly imputation technique that improves IoT data availability by imputing anomalous sensor data" (p. 194). As for yearly productivity, only 1 article was published every year between 2012 and 2022. Five articles were published in 2015; 13 in 2016, 13 in 2017, and 28 in 2018. In 2019, 34 articles were published, 48 articles in 2020, 69 articles in 2021, and by July 2020, 51 articles. The annual trends in publications on this subject are shown in Fig. (**1**) and were derived from a sample of 694 articles. With 126 papers published, 2019 marked the highest number of publications. Additionally, as data gathering began in September 2020 and the subject is expanding, more articles are anticipated to have been published in 2020 than in 2019. Many publications on biometric voting using IoT to transfer vote to centralized system that have been published over time will be analyzed, and the study will be furthered to reveal data that will permit a better understanding of earlier studies' applicability.

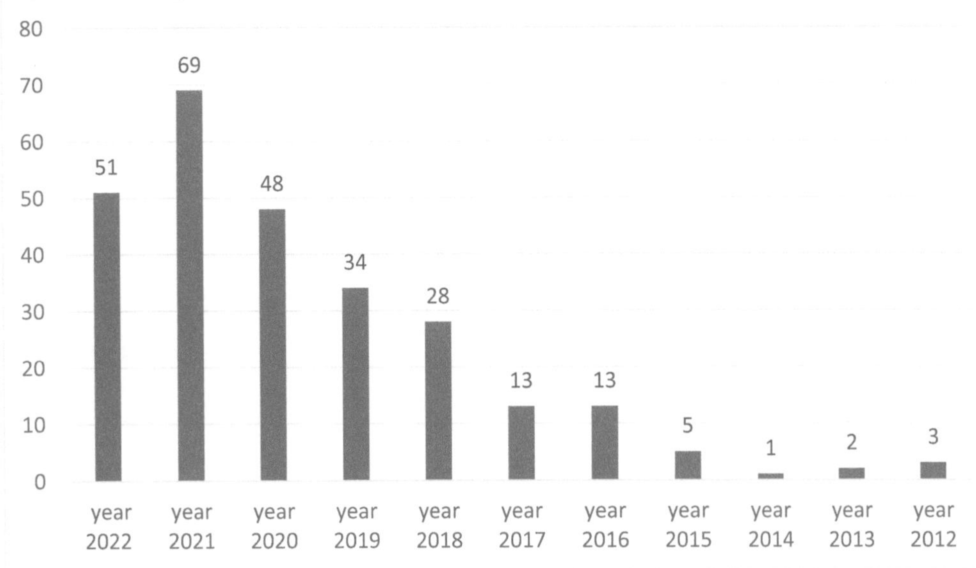

Fig (1). Publication by year.

The 19 subject areas listed in Table **1** are used to categorize the 267 articles. With 225 related articles, or 84.270 percent of the total, the subject field "Computer Science" is the dominant subject area. Engineering, with 115 articles, is the second subject area with the greatest number of related articles, followed by "Decision Sciences," with 45 articles. It is vital to remember that a single article might be categorized under multiple headings, which can affect both total and partial statistics.

Table 1. Number of publications by category.

Scopus Subject Area	**Number**	**% of 267**
Computer Science	225	84.270
Engineering	115	43.071
Decision Sciences	45	16.854
Mathematics	43	16.105
Physics and Astronomy	24	8.989
Materials Science	16	5.993
Business, Management and Accounting	15	5.618
Medicine	13	4.869
Social Sciences	13	4.869
Energy	7	2.622

(Table 1) cont.....

Scopus Subject Area	Number	% of 267
Biochemistry, Genetics and Molecular Biology	6	2.247
Chemistry	6	2.247
Multidisciplinary	3	1.124
Chemical Engineering	2	0.749
Neuroscience	2	0.749
Arts and Humanities	1	0.375
Earth and Planetary Sciences	1	0.375
Economics, Econometrics and Finance	1	0.375
Environmental Science	1	0.375

Articles by Journal. The 267 publications were published in 161 distinct journals, according to our analysis of the journals (Table **2**).

Table 2. Productivity of journals summary (2012 - 2022).

Production Volume by Journal	Journals	% of 161
17 articles published	1	0.621
10 articles published	1	0.621
9 articles published	1	0.621
8 articles published	2	1.242
6 articles published	2	1.242
4 articles published	2	1.242
3 articles published	7	4.348
2 articles published	20	12.422
1 article published	125	77.640
Total	161	100

Out of 161 journals, 77.640% published simply 1 article on the topic researched, which is an indicator that these journals are not from the biometric voting area using IoT to transfer votes to a central system; 12.422% (20 journals) published only 2 articles; 4.348% (7 journals) published 3 articles; 1.242% (2 journals) of 4 articles published; 1.242% (2 journals) of six articles published; 1.242% (2 journals) of eight articles; 0.621% (1 journal) published nine articles; 0.621% (1 journals) published ten articles and 0.621% (1 journals) published seventeen articles. They can be considered journals of biometric voting using IoT to transfer votes to a central system as they published more than one article (Table **2**). Additionally, we can see in Fig. (**2**) how interdisciplinary this study topic is and how it may be published in journals from other domains and using various methodologies. Fig. (**2**) presents journals with more than three publications relating to biometric voting using IoT to transfer votes to a central system.

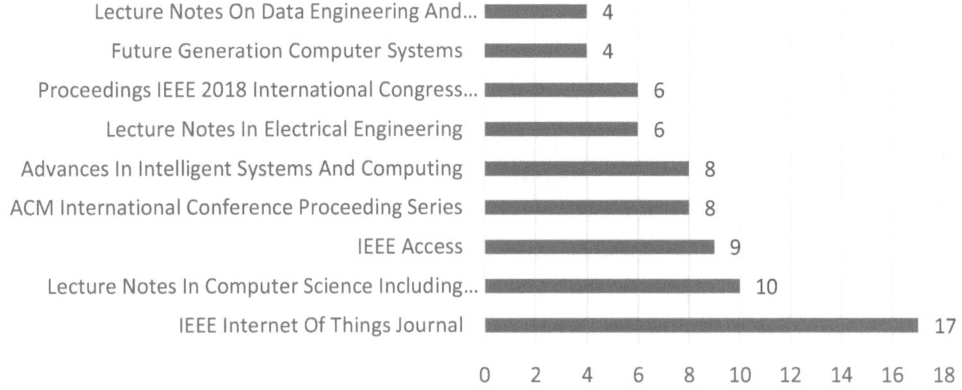

Fig. (2). Publications by year (2012 - 2022).

As shown in Table **3**, we looked at 9 journals that have 4 or more publications on the topic. These journals published 72 articles, accounting for 26.366 percent of the sample articles. As can be seen, "IEEE Internet of Things Journal" has the most articles published (17 articles altogether), accounting for 6.367 percent of the sample as a whole, followed by the "Lecture Notes in Computer Science including Subseries Lecture Notes in Artificial Intelligence and Lecture Notes in Bioinformatics" with 3.745 percent (10 articles).

Table 3. Publications of journal (2012 - 2022).

Publication by Journal	Number	% of 267
IEEE Internet of Things Journal	17	6.367
Lecture Notes In Computer Science Including Subseries Lecture Notes in Artificial Intelligence And Lecture Notes in Bioinformatics	10	3.745
IEEE Access	9	3.371
ACM International Conference Proceeding Series	8	2.996
Advances In Intelligent Systems and Computing	8	2.996
Lecture Notes in Electrical Engineering	6	2.247
Proceedings IEEE 2018 International Congress on Cybermatics 2018 IEEE Conferences on Internet of Things Green Computing and Communications Cyber Physical and Social Computing Smart Data Blockchain Computer and Information Technology things Greencom Cpscom Smart data Blockchain CIT 2018	6	2.247

(Table 3) cont.....

Publication by Journal	Number	% of 267
Future Generation Computer Systems	4	1.498
Lecture Notes on Data Engineering and Communications Technologies	4	1.498

Keyword Analysis

The 267 items in the sample were categorized using the most popular keywords that were found and examined. The subjects that come up more frequently in the analyzed area stand out as a result of this analysis. The map shown in Fig. (**3**) organizes the keywords into 55 groupings. The internet of things, blockchain, and security are further highlighted in this map as areas where new research possibilities may be developing.

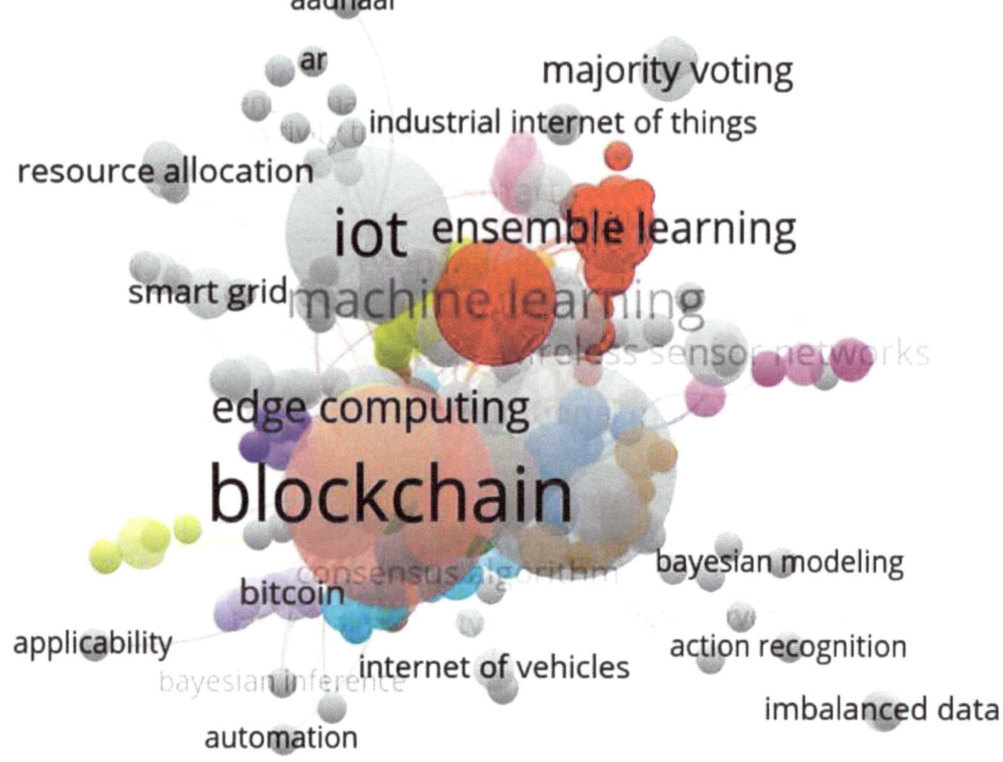

Fig. (3). Keyword trends (2012 - 2022).

From the 267 articles, 831 keywords were recognized. Of these, we present three of the most frequent keywords. The keyword "Internet of things" has an occurrence in 97 articles, being the word that is used most often to summarize the analyzed articles' key subjects, which means 11.673% prevalence with the highest overall link strength of 551 (Table **4**). Blockchain appeared fifty-one times with the second highest overall link strength of 234, equivalent to 6.137%; and security was recognized as a minimum of 18 articles, *i.e.,* 1.16% with an overall link strength of 133. The keywords "Internet of things", "Blockchain", "Security", "Machine learning", "Voting", "Smart contract", "Electronic voting", "Edge computing", "Ensemble learning" and "e-voting" appeared more than six times.

Table 4. Ten most occurred keywords.

Keyword	Occurrence	Total Link Strength
Internet of things	97	551
Blockchain	51	234
Security	18	133
Machine learning	17	120
Voting	11	64
Smart contract	11	54
Electronic voting	10	50
Edge computing	8	53
Ensemble learning	8	44
e-voting	7	39

Geographical Analysis of Publications

The 267 publications that make up the sample are spread across 71 different nations, indicating that this study issue is international when the country of affiliation of the authors is examined. This indicates that each of these nations has at least one article published. The five nations with the greatest number of scholarly articles on biometric voting using the Internet of Things to transfer votes to a central system are listed in Table **5**. They account for 72.285 percent of all articles published collectively. The findings show that China, with 74 articles, 590 citations, and 49 total link strengths, has the largest number of publications, citations, and overall link strength. This is followed by India with 60 articles, 284 citations and 27 total link strength. The United States of America is in 3rd place in publication with 34 articles, 253 citations, and 23 total link strengths (Table **5**).

Table 5. Publications in co-authorship by country (2012 - 2022).

Co-authorship by Countries	Number	Citations	Total Link Strength
China	74	590	49
India	60	284	27
United States of America	34	253	23
South Korea	13	97	5
Saudi Arabia	12	44	18

The national co-authorship map from the sample of 267 articles is shown in Fig. (**4**). The group of nations consisting of China, India, the United States of America, South Korea, and Saudi Arabia may be seen. The distance between the clusters on the map and the lines connecting them illustrates the intensity of the relationships between the countries and how frequently they publish as co-authors. This is a good indication of the strength of international cooperation in the biometric voting field using IoT to transfer votes to a central system of research.

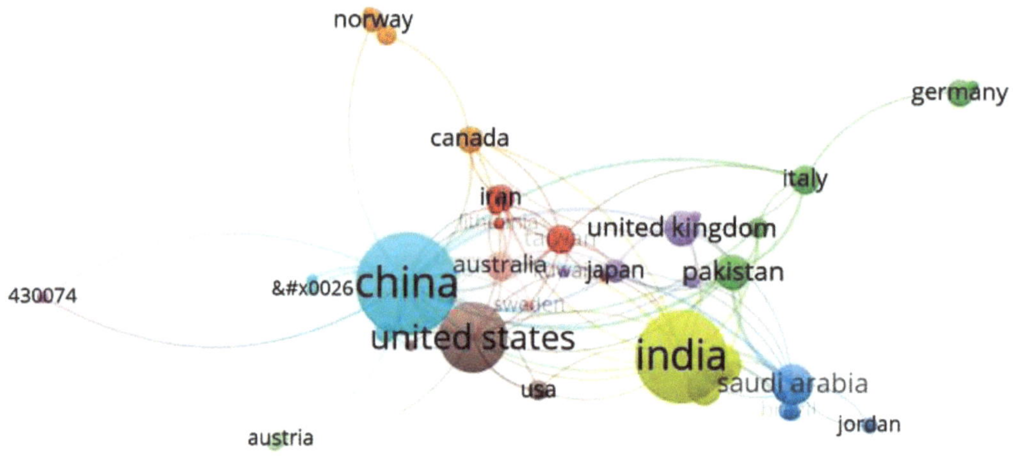

Fig. (4). Publications in co-authorship by country (2012 - 2022).

Publications Analysis by Organization

The top six universities accountable for the 267 articles' publications are Beijing Jiaotong University, China University of Technology and Mining, Zhejiang University, Norwegian University of Technology and Science, Sri Krishna College of Technology, and Sungkyunkwan University. However, it is obvious that the occurrences are extremely dispersed concerning papers' volumes produced by an organization, unlike what occurs in journals or nations of publication. With three publications each, or 1.124 percent of the 267 articles, the Information and Electronic Engineering School and the University of Beijing Jiaotong tied for first place. The six organizations that have generated the most scholarly publications in the field of research are listed in Table **6**.

Table 6. Publications by organizations.

Organization	Number	% of 267
Beijing jiaotong university	3	1.124
China university of mining and technology	2	0.749
Zhejiang university	2	0.749
Norwegian university of science and technology	2	0.749
Sri Krishna college of technology	2	0.749
Sungkyunkwan university	2	0.749

The key universities that have published publications on biometric voting using IoT to transfer vote to a centralized system, as well as the collaboration between the institutions, are displayed on the map created by the VOSviewer program (Fig. **5**). The sample of 267 articles used in this research was used to create the aforementioned map.

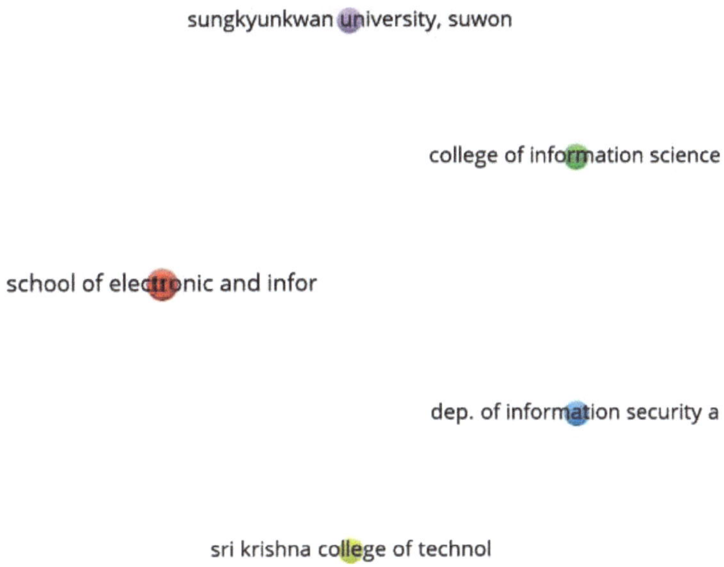

Fig. (5). Publications by organization.

It is feasible to determine the publishers' organizations and the relationships among them by analyzing Fig. (**5**). In the Scopus-generated results shown in Fig. (**5**), we can find Beijing Jiaotong University without its School of Electrical and Information Engineering. as well as the Control and Information Engineering School at the China University of Technology and Mining, the College of Electronic Engineering and Information Science at Zhejiang University, the Department of Communication Technology and Information Security at the Norwegian University of Technology and Science, and others.

Analysis of Citations

Since it identifies the important papers in the field of study, the analysis of article citations is the most popular technique for evaluating the influence of authors, journals, and articles [23]. Table **7** examines the citation structure in the pertinent field of study. The reference publication, "Hybrid of anomaly-based and specification-based IDS for the Internet of Things utilizing unsupervised OPF based on the MapReduce technique," has a total of 120 citations, making it easy to see which works are most frequently cited in this field.

Table 7. Citations by articles with the highest citation.

Title	Authors	Journal
Hybrid of anomaly-based and specification-based IDS for Internet of Things using unsupervised OPF based on MapReduce approach	Hamid, B. and Mansour, S.	Computer Communications
AI-based two-stage intrusion detection for software defined IoT networks	Jiaqi, L.; Zhifeng, Z.; Rongpeng, L.; Honggang, Z.	IEEE Internet of Things Journal
Blockchain trust model for malicious node detection in wireless sensor networks	Wei, S.; Qi, L.; Zhao, T.; Jian-Sen, C.; Bo, W. and Wei, L.	IEEE Access
The survey on near field communication	Vedat, C.; Busra, O. and Kerem, O.	Sensors (Switzerland)

(Table 7) cont.....

Title	Authors	Journal
Astraea: A Decentralized Blockchain Oracle	John, A.; Ryan, B.; Andreas, V.; Zissis, P.; Neil, V. and Anastasia, K.	Proceedings - IEEE 2018 International Congress on Cybermatics: 2018 IEEE Conferences on Internet of Things, Green Computing and Communications, Cyber, Physical and Social Computing, Smart Data, Blockchain, Computer and Information Technology, iThings/GreenCom/CPSCom/SmartData/Blockchain/CIT 2018
E-Voting with Blockchain: An E-Voting Protocol with Decentralisation and Voter Privacy	Sheer, H.F.; Apostolos, G.; Naeem, A.R. and Konstantinos, M.	Proceedings - IEEE 2018 International Congress on Cybermatics: 2018 IEEE Conferences on Internet of Things, Green Computing and Communications, Cyber, Physical and Social Computing, Smart Data, Blockchain, Computer and Information Technology, iThings/GreenCom/CPSCom/SmartData/Blockchain/CIT 2018
Large-scale Election Based on Blockchain	Baocheng, W.; Jiawei, S.; Yunhua, H.; Dandan, P. and Ningxiao, L.	Procedia Computer Science

Researchers can find the foundational content that can be utilized as their studies' support reference by understanding the most-cited publications, giving them an obvious place to start. It is feasible to determine the author citation network by looking at Fig. (**6**). When two documents make reference to the same document, a citation is generated. This method is used to illustrate a document's applicability to a specific topic area and is applied to papers, journals, and authors. Along with other names like Song, J. and Cho, S.H., the red cluster of authors most frequently mentioned includes the Chinese author Wang, Y. from Beijing Jiaotong University.

Fig (6). Author citation network.

Analysis by Author

The last analysis discusses publication and author production. The most prolific author is shown in Table **8**. Chinese professor Wang, Yipeng from Information and Electronic Engineering School, University of Beijing Jiaotong, Beijing, China has nine of the 267 publications with 29 total link strength, followed by the

Chinese authors Liu, Yizhi from China University of Geosciences, Zhang, H. from Army Engineering University of Pla and Yang, W. from Beijing Jiaotong University.

Table 8. Publication by authors.

Author	Number	Total Link Strength
Wang Y.	7	29
Liu, X.	5	19
Zhang, H.	5	17
Yang, W.	5	14

When two documents quote the same source, this is known as bibliographic coupling, which can show how strong a certain publication is in comparison to other publications' group. This method can be used with articles, journals, writers, institutions, and nations. It is feasible to identify the articles and writers who are frequently cited by looking at the authors' bibliographic coupling. Authors' bibliographic coupling is represented in Fig. (7), which enables us to see and gauge the strength of the relationship between them. The map shows fifteen clearly identified clusters, and the connected lines provide author citations.

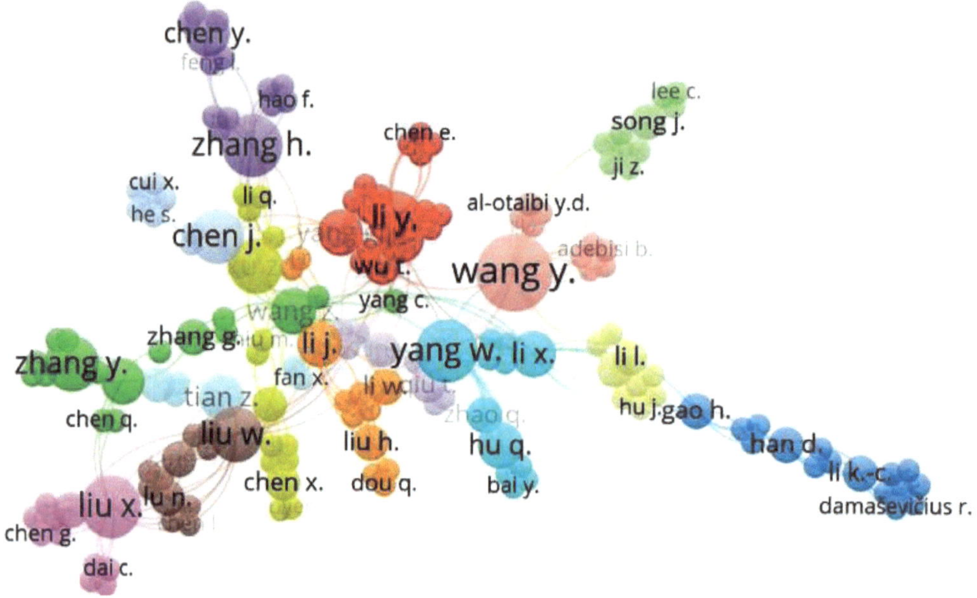

Fig. (7). Author citation network.

Analysis of Research Opportunities

This study's objective is to highlight the key research possibilities in this area, as well as give a research overview and the investigation directions on biometric voting utilizing IoT to transfer votes to a central system. As a result, the purpose of this section is to evaluate and suggest future possibilities for research in this area based on content analysis. The review of eight of the most recent and pertinent publications recommended by Scopus led to the selection of the eight papers shown in Table 7. They were thought to be the most mentioned and pertinent because they were published during the last five years. Although blockchain technology holds a lot of promise, its existing limitations may prevent it from realizing its full potential. Research on the fundamentals of blockchain technology needs to be intensified in order to enhance its capabilities and support for sophisticated apps that can run on the network of the blockchain. The voting procedure can be made considerably simpler in future studies by using other means for verification, for example, the fingerprint sensors found in phones.

DISCUSSION

The current study contributes to our understanding of the state-of-the-art in studies on biometric voting that uses IoT to convey votes to a central system. It is useful to discover the nations and organizations that publish the most in journals, with a focus on biometric voting utilizing IoT. In particular, the significance of publications from the co-citation networks, trends in the covered themes centered on keywords, and transfer votes to the central system As a result, it is crucial to identify knowledge gaps in this domain and potential future trends in research. This study analyzes the top journals, writers, keywords, and institutions, demonstrating that (a) the body of knowledge on using IoT to transfer votes to a central system *via* biometric voting is rapidly expanding. (b) Eight publications alone accounted for 60 or more citations, and a sizable portion of the study was written by a number of prolific authors. (c) Of the 267 publications included in this review, 26.066 percent were found in primary sources. (d) China is the top nation with regard to citations and documents. Finally, this area of the literature on biometric voting has a lot of potential and is predicted to increase significantly over the next few years. The outcomes show a clear trend as a result of the increased emphasis on biometric voting. People are more concerned about the effectiveness of the electronic voting system for smooth and peaceful elections. Individuals wish to understand the direct voting impact on society. Therefore, since people are more aware of election problems, the study of biometric voting using IoT to transfer votes to a central system can help businesses, governments, and countries have effective and peaceful elections. To establish clear and long-lasting biometric voting methods, it is crucial to understand the different types of electronic voting and the advantages and disadvantages they provide. It is crucial to involve all interested parties in the development of effective biometric voting, including local government, people, and public and private service providers. The studies of biometric voting by Othman *et al.* and Mallikarjuna *et al.* make important contributions. Customers and other stakeholders have become significant players in the chain of sustainable tourism. As more parties become involved in this process, the development of biometric voting solutions may actually contribute to and benefit from peaceful elections. Implantable sensors are permanently implanted inside the human body by SS singh *et. al.* The implantation process of these sensors necessitates a surgical operation. Due to the complexity and precision required, the proper implantation of these sensors calls for the expertise of skilled surgeons. Traffic sign recognition is to develop a deep neural network (DNN) capable of accurately classifying traffic signs. The authors propose training the model using the German Traffic Sign Dataset, enabling it to interpret and recognize traffic signs within natural images effectively.

CONCLUSION

By giving information on the current state of the art and classifying gaps, trends, and research opportunities through content analysis and the most pertinent and recent publications' selection published in this field of research, the current study adds to the body of existing research. The public and service institutions make up the government sector. Through a web system connected to IoT devices, citizens can easily participate in elections or referendums. This allows them to simply express their ideas and acquire the results of elections or referendums promptly, correctly, and without duplicate votes. The system uses the blockchain to preserve and maintain the privacy of the citizens' data. Only adults or those who are entitled to vote may cast ballots when logging in to vote. After entering his or her personal information and electoral card number, the citizen's data is checked and cross-referenced with the government's database of citizen records. In order to cast a ballot in a governmental election, a voter must visit one of the many voting machines that are located throughout the country after completing the online voting process to verify his vote using his fingerprint, which would then be compared to previously recorded information about him in the government's database of voter records. Only governmental elections require this fingerprint verification technique. With fingerprint verification's exception to speed up the process of voting since it is not as crucial as elections, the voting process in referendums or governmental surveys is the same as in governmental voting elections. By matching the data entered with the database of the government's citizen records, the voter's information is verified. Instead, the private sector, which consists of organizations or businesses that work in the social sector, wants to hold a referendum or create surveys to get the views of the public. They can organize referendums, and the system aids in gathering opinions from citizens in a timely and accurate manner. Without going through the verification and confirmation processes required for voting in the public sector, citizens can access the website directly to complete the questionnaire and cast their votes. Because it is a standard procedure, the person's identification does not need to be verified or confirmed. The group or establishment that organized the poll or referendum can quickly obtain the voting results. Each vote, if it is for public or private voting, triggers the creation of a new node in the blockchain by the smart contract. The vote is then recorded in the database, guaranteeing that it is secure from tampering or fraud. One can highlight further contributions made by the current study. First, a description of the evolution of the terminology employed in this field of study. The most common terms used to refer to studies on biometric voting using IoT to transfer votes to a central system are "Internet of Things" first, followed by "blockchain." Understanding the growing interest in the study of biometric voting using the Internet of Things to convey votes to a central system is the foundation of a second contribution. The number of publications has increased over the past ten years, from 3 articles in 2012 to 267 articles as of 2022, demonstrating the expanding tendency in this field of study. The keyword clusters seen with VOSviewer indicate a rise over time. Such increasing interest clearly indicates the effects of biometric voting using IoT and its results, as well as the prospective paths of future research. The categorization and source of relevant research are shown as a third contribution. The most prevalent subject area overall is "Computer Science," with 225 related articles, or 84.270 percent of the 267 articles, demonstrating publications' significant predominance in specialized biometric voting journals. The research centers on around 71 nations that collectively comprise 100% of the articles published, with China leading the pack with 74 publications. Fourthly, the paper helps identify the journals that publish the research majority that falls under the chosen criteria. With 17 articles, or 6.367 percent of the publications, the IEEE Internet of Things Journal is at the top of the list. Lecture Notes in Computer Science, including Lecture Notes in Bioinformatics and Subseries, published 10 papers, accounting for 3.745 percent of all papers published. Lecture Notes in Artificial Intelligence comes in second. The research concludes with the most pertinent and recent articles' content study, examining the locations and subjects under consideration that appear to be more well-liked as well as the general directions under investigation. This work could provide invaluable hints to individuals looking into or planning to explore this field of inquiry. Future studies can look into various points of view regarding the viability of biometric voting. Another development is comparative studies in the area of electronic voting. The most intriguing issues in this area appear to be those involving various situations, particular destinations, the major roles of citizens, and their perspectives. It is likewise recommended that voting variables be addressed in particular research bibliometric, looking at their association with IoT variables in academic literature as part of future research. Another recommendation for bibliometric future analyses might be to address a potential cybersecurity risk in academic research's creation in the electronic voting area, against the backdrop of a pandemic that restricts people's ability to move around locally and globally, making it more difficult to vote. The findings for the year 2022 are only valid up to the month of July, which is when the data collection was done. To give a comprehensive account of scientific output in 2022, future studies may cover the entire year. The bibliometric analysis is dependent on technical choices, such as selecting a research and language area, which may exclude important works. Another drawback is that, after consulting alternative databases, it was determined to only use Scopus. A multisource approach comparing several databases could provide a thorough review of the research in this area and a clearer understanding of the key distinctions and implications of using various databases. The ability of bibliometric analysis to analyze the contexts and drivers of citation activity is restricted. A bibliometric technique offers an analysis that is primarily descriptive and might not include enough content analysis to improve the capacity of explanation and offer a deeper examination of the findings and consequences.

REFERENCES

[1] S. Nižetić, P. Šolić, D. López-de-Ipiña González-de-Artaza, and L. Patrono, "Internet of Things (IoT): Opportunities, issues and challenges towards a smart and sustainable future", *J. Clean. Prod.*, vol. 274, p. 122877, 2020.
[http://dx.doi.org/10.1016/j.jclepro.2020.122877] [PMID: 32834567]

[2] D. Khoury, E.F. Kfoury, A. Kassem, and H. Harb, "Decentralized voting platform based on ethereum blockchain", 2018 IEEE *Int. Multidiscip. Conf. Eng. Technol. IMCET,* Beirut, Lebanon, pp. 1-6, 2018.
[http://dx.doi.org/10.1109/IMCET.2018.8603050]

[3] R.K. Geetanjali, and R. Naveen, "An enhanced security mechanism through blockchain for E-polling / counting process using IoT devices", *Wirel. Netw.,* vol. 5, 2019.
[http://dx.doi.org/10.1007/s11276-019-02112-5]

[4] S. Shukla, A.N. Thasmiya, D.O. Shashank, and H.R. Mamatha, "Online Voting Application Using", *2018 Int. Conf. Adv. Comput. Commun. Informatics* September 2018, Indi Bangalore, pp. 873-880.
[http://dx.doi.org/10.1109/ICACCI.2018.8554652]

[5] L. Christian Schaupp, and L. Carter, "E-voting: From apathy to adoption", *J. Enterp. Inf. Manag.,* vol. 18, no. 5, pp. 586-601, 2005.
[http://dx.doi.org/10.1108/17410390510624025]

[6] W.D. Eggers, *Government 2.0: Using technology to improve education, cut red tape, reduce gridlock, and enhance democracy.* Rowman & Littlefield, 2007.

[7] T.M. Harrison, T.A. Pardo, and M. Cook, "Creating open government ecosystems: A research and development agenda", *Future Internet,* vol. 4, no. 4, pp. 900-928, 2012.

[http://dx.doi.org/10.3390/fi4040900]

[8] K-H. Wang, S.K. Mondal, K. Chan, and X. Xie, "A review of contemporary e-voting: Requirements, technology, systems and usability", *Data Science and Pattern Recognition,* vol. 1, no. 1, pp. 31-47, 2017.

[9] D.A. Gritzalis, "Principles and requirements for a secure e-voting system", *Comput. Secur.,* vol. 21, no. 6, pp. 539-556, 2002. [http://dx.doi.org/10.1016/S0167-4048(02)01014-3]

[10] R. Anane, R. Freeland, and G. Theodoropoulos, E-voting requirements and implementation. *The 9th IEEE CEC/EEE 2007.* IEEE, 2007, pp. 382-392.

[11] Available from: https://www.businessinsider.com/internet-of-things-report

[12] J.R. Gil-Garcia, T.A. Pardo, and M. Gasco-Hernandez, Internet of things and the public sector.*Beyond Smart and Connected Governments.* Springer, 2020, pp. 3-24. [http://dx.doi.org/10.1007/978-3-030-37464-8_1]

[13] A. Berentsen, *Aleksander Berentsen Recommends 'Bitcoin: A peer-to-peer electronic cash system' by satoshi nakamoto. in 21st century economics.* Springer, 2019, pp. 7-8.

[15] K. Srikrishnaswetha, S. Kumar, and R. Mahmood, *A study on smart electronics voting machine using face recognition and aadhar verification with IOT.* Springer Singapore, 2019, pp. 67-95. [http://dx.doi.org/10.1007/978-981-13-3765-9_10]

[16] M.V. Varalakshmi, S. Malarvizhi, A. Shamitha, S. Srimathi, and V. Vinisha, "Blockvote: Aadhar based electronic voting system using blockchain", *Int. J. Sci. Res. Eng. Dev.,* vol. 3, no. 3, pp. 421-427, 2020.

[17] F. Garrigos-Simon, Y. Narangajavana-Kaosiri, and I. Lengua-Lengua, "Tourism and sustainability: A bibliometric and visualization analysis", *Sustainability,* vol. 10, no. 6, p. 1976, 2018. [http://dx.doi.org/10.3390/su10061976]

[18] C. Mulet-Forteza, O. Martorell-Cunill, J.M. Merigó, J. Genovart-Balaguer, and E. Mauleon-Mendez, "Twenty five years of the Journal of Travel & Tourism Marketing : A bibliometric ranking", *J. Travel Tour. Mark.,* vol. 35, no. 9, pp. 1201-1221, 2018. [http://dx.doi.org/10.1080/10548408.2018.1487368]

[19] L. Li, H. Wang, Y. Wang, M. Chen, and T. Wei, "Improving IoT data availability *via* feedback- and voting-based anomaly imputation", *Future Gener. Comput. Syst.,* vol. 135, pp. 194-204, 2022. [http://dx.doi.org/10.1016/j.future.2022.04.027]

[20] A.A. Othman, E.A. Muhammed, H.K. Mujahid, H.A. Muhammed, and M.A. Mosleh, "Online voting system based on iot and ethereum blockchain", *2021 International Conference of Technology, Science and Administration (ICTSA)* 22-24 March 2021, Taiz, Yemen, 2021, pp. 1-6. [http://dx.doi.org/10.1109/ICTSA52017.2021.9406528]

[21] B. Mallikarjuna, K. Sathish, J. Gitanjali, and P.V. Krishna, "An efficient vote casting system with Aadhar verification through blockchain", *Inter. J. System Systems Eng.,* vol. 11, no. 3/4, pp. 237-256, 2021. [http://dx.doi.org/10.1504/IJSSE.2021.121439]

[22] S.S. Kshatri, D. Bhonsle, S. Tiwari, R. Mishra, T. Rizvi, and R. Pandey, *Sensor-based devices and their applications in smart healthcare systems.* IOP Publishing: OP ebooks. Bristol, UK, 2022. [http://dx.doi.org/10.1088/978-0-7503-5326-7ch9]

[23] M. Nayak, "An AI-Based efficient model for the classification of traffic signals using convolutional neural network building secure business models through blockchain technology: Tactics", In: *Building Secure Business Models Through Blockchain Technology: Tactics, Methods, Limitations, and Performance* Methods, Limitations, and Performance Copyright, 2023, p. 16. [http://dx.doi.org/10.4018/978-1-6684-7808-0.ch002]

CHAPTER 5

Face Recognition using Convolutional Neural Network Algorithms

Eram Fatima[1,*], **Ankit Kumar**[1] and **Anil Kumar Singh**[1]

[1] *Department of Information Technology, Babu Banarasi Das Institute of Technology and Management, Lucknow, India*

Abstract: Biometric applications have massive demand in today's era. The areas of applications are mostly linked with the security of the system. Biometric features are regarded as the primary resource for security purposes due to their own distinctiveness and non-volatile essence. System authentication using biometrics is considered to be a sophisticated technology. Noise effect inducts variation in the biometric subject that causes an adverse impact on establishing the recognition. The proposed model supported the development of an effective method for performing facial biometric feature recognition. The model's goal is to reduce the number of false approvals and refusals. The proposed algorithm has been applied over a video dataset containing surveillance video frames that capture facial subjects dynamically. The first step is the pre-processing of the video frames that have been carried out in the proposed model. Then, the Viola-Jones algorithm was applied to detect the facial subjects in the video frames. Feature extraction from the facial subject has been accomplished by applying a deep reinforcement learning algorithm. Further, the proposed model applied a convolutional neural network (CNN) algorithm to perform feature recognition of facial identity accurately. The proposed technique aims to maintain a huge recognition rate of dynamic facial subjects under various unprecedented noise variations. In the classification algorithm, the recognition accuracy is found to be 98.85%.

Keywords: Convolution neural network, Deep reinforcement, Face recognition, Pre-processing learning.

INTRODUCTION

Any individual's biometric features contain extremely important information. System authentication that uses biometric features is pretty common and reliable nowadays; even so, due to vulnerabilities in communication systems, such features can be hijacked or bypassed by an imposter to establish redundant authentication in the system. Biometric identity is a type of user's permanent and

* **Corresponding author Eram Fatima:** Department of Information Technology, Babu Banarasi Das Institute of Technology and Management, Lucknow, India; E-mail: Eramf9@gmail.com

Suman Kumar Swarnkar, Sapna Singh Kshatri, Virendra Kumar Swarnkar & Tien Anh Tran (Eds.)

unique identity that is used to keep the user's authentication secure. Within an image's areas, segmentation divides it into elements or artifacts. It is an important instrument for the processing of facial images as described by Rafael & Richard (2017) [1]. Segmentation is an important method for radiological assessment or computer-aided diagnosis in most medical image processing and classification. Face detection and recognition seem to be useful in a wide variety of video processing application fields, including user authentication, video forensic investigations, as well as a wide range of many other video processing applications. The recognition rate may be negatively affected if facial features are read within the less-quality frames in the video [2]. It speeds up the feature learning process in models where feature statistics aren't efficient enough to guarantee exact recognition. The given paper uses deep reinforcement learning with the CNN algorithm to tackle the issues of low-quality video data. Different layers of CNN effectively analyze a video's low-quality frame. The CNN classifier accomplishes the goal of facial image classification using extracted features. The work's major contribution is that it continues to attain face recognition using dynamic video input instead of static pictures. This same video data is adopted from the chokepoint dataset [3], which is a standard database. This paper employs the concepts of Viola Jones, pre-processing, deep reinforcement learning, as well as CNN to efficiently implement face recognition. This work aims to contribute by detecting and identifying the facial subject from video input under relatively undiscovered circumstances including poor illumination, noise, blurring, different poses, angles, changing expressions, and so on. Over the past few decades, the utilization of artificial intelligence (AI) and deep learning (DL) has consistently risen. Studies centered on convolutional neural networks (CNNs) have gained significant prominence, given their effectiveness in analyzing images and other forms of structured data. CNNs are widely regarded as a powerful tool in this regard [4].

The goal of this research is to reduce error rates (FAR and FRR) under various image processing threats. The model's reliability for vibrant input, including such video data, is confirmed by this work [5]. A specific video frame can sometimes contain images of multiple individuals, making it difficult for any basic model to identify and recognize each face individually. The suggested model performs exceptionally well in a frame of multiple faces while retaining high recognition accuracy. The remaining modules are arranged as follows: Module II demonstrates the proposed methodology. Module III contains the results of the experiment. The conclusion/proposal will be summarized in last section. References are kept in the final module.

PROPOSED METHODOLOGY

The suggested method collects data of video with a video recorder on the inside of any room which records distinct individuals who enters the room. A few video frames of data input comprise various images of the same person. These video frames are then analyzed to see if each user's face can be recognized. Fig. (**1**) shows sample input video dataset [5].

Fig. (1). Frames from the input video.

As shown in the diagram above, several people have indeed managed to capture throughout video frames. The image resolution is 552X480 pixels and the frame rate is 30 frames per second. The dataset contains 48 video sequences and 64,204 face images in total.

Viola Jones

A system with the efficiency to detect objects in real time can able to fetch a portion of the facial subject of individuals from the input video. One of these kinds of systems termed as "Viola Jones" has been utilized in the proposed solution. To find facial portions throughout video frames, the model uses the Viola-Jones scheme, which detects features of haar from facial portions [6]. These characteristics are indistinguishable from one another and are unaffected by noise, poor lighting, an abnormal expression, or even the pose of an individual in the recorded video frame. The algorithm tracks the subject's face by scanning every one of the video frames' situated feature points and enclosing it in a rectangular surrounding. The area of a rectangular surrounding has been computed and compared to the sum of the values of each feature point to generate Haar feature points. A few video frame samples of the extricated facial subjects have been presented in Fig. (**2**).

Fig. (2). Few Faces extracted from video input samples.

Viola Jones Algorithm

Input:- Images from the recorded video frame
Output:- Face subject from the entire image
Step 1:- Input image

$I(Q) = \sum_{k=0} \sum_{j=0}^{i} yz$

Step 2:- Q, the set of positive windows declared by cascade
Set B = {[k,k+e-1]} * [j, j+e-1] € N
For M =1 to M do, 0<y<=1
Every window in R do
End
Step 3:-*Normalize the weight*

$$W_k = \frac{W_k}{\sum k W_k}$$

If $e/W_k > 0.4$ then
Return true
Else return false
End if
Step 5:- Return R

Deep Reinforcement

Deep reinforcement learning allows a system to learn from its own feedback. The current proposal helps in extracting the HOG features from the fetched facial data by applying Viola-Jones algorithm that are then converted into a binary representation in the form of tree. To generate similar binary codes, numerous occurring features from multiple facial images of a single person are used. Each of the featured facial subjects was mapped to a binary tree that was similar [7]. A single person entering multiple times in video frames could be captured using the proposed model. Deep reinforcement learning is being used in this case to create a new binary tree for different frames, which usually contains the same person who enters numerous times. The goal of the algorithm is to increase this same number of binary trees for various persons videoed. So, every binary code segment recognizes just one related facial subject which is distinguishable from the other facial subjects' binary codes. The question arises of whether the ensemble of SVM classifiers can outperform individual SVM classifiers in terms of the number of positive and negative predictions [8]. The hashing function is used as an agent in the proposed system to convert hog features into the fixed-size binary codes. All of the hash codes have been generated as a means of maximizing the re-ward. In binary codes, there could be some mistakes [9]. As a result, a back- propagation technique has been used in deep reinforcement learning to send the hash codes return to a previous state, in which the weights of the agent function have been updated to generate the most effective reward. Those images that depict a single person have been plotted to binary codes that are similar. The CNN model eventually uses the resulting binary codes to recognize the user's faces and correctly classifies the images. The strategy network in Fig. (**3**) is by far the most important part of deep reinforcement learning because it uses the try and error interactions method to learn the binary tree.

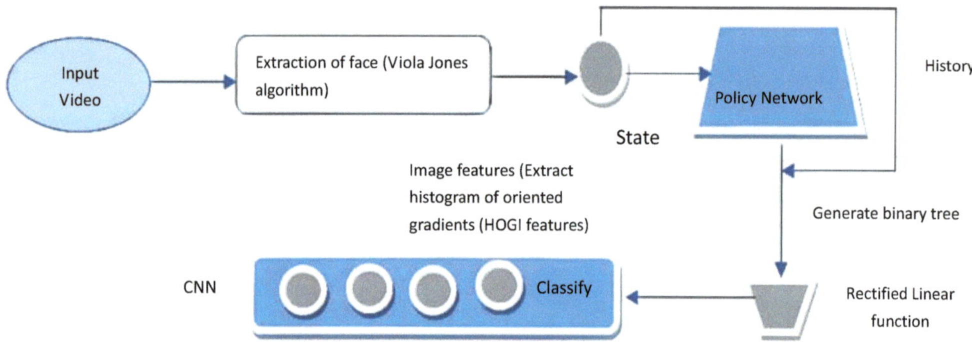

Fig. (3). Flowchart of the proposed face recognition model.

The static framework recorded in the image's left-most part. This is a 224×224×3 two-dimensional state. The system generates 5 three-dimensional frames: three 112×112×128 frames and two 224×224×64 frames. In the same way, several dimensional frames are chosen for the next step. The above equation is an equation of single perceptron in the CNN model. It states that the summation of the product of weights and the input vectors are carried out along with a default input (Bias input) in order to ignite the functioning of the perceptron.

Deep reinforcement learning algorithm

Total number of extracted faces as an input
Total binary trees generated as an output
Step 1:- Set the value of A to zero.

Step 2:- While A is not converged do s←(Z,b)
r'←(Z,b)
Step 3:- For

Using the policy divided from A, choose B and Z.
Take action B and observe R, Z
$R(Z) = \sum_{m=0}^{m} \sum_{n}^{n} xs$, $0 < x <= 1$
Where $s = A(r', b) - Q(r, b)$
Receive reward R_c and new state Z_{c+1}
c←c+1
$A_0, (Z_0, b_0) \leftarrow A_0 (Z, b) + x \ R_m$

End

$$y_{ij} = \sigma\left(\sum_{a=0}^{m-1} \sum_{b=0}^{m-1} w_{ab} x_{(i+a)(j+b)}\right)$$

Convolutional Neural Network (CNN)

This algorithm uses a deep network to take an input signal and assign weights and biases to it, followed by organizing each neuron's connection to another neuron. The interlinking of hidden layers has been done in the same way. The model is used to control the functionality by adjusting the weights and numerical multiple functionalities. CNN gains an advantage mostly in small and simple architectural designs when dealing with integrative situations. The information conveyed from input passed through different layers is assigned specific weights that are multiplied by 0 or 1, and if the system is unable to recognize a pattern, a mathematically controlled flow chart is used to deal with the situation. The neural network used in the proposed model ensures the following characteristics. For the training model, 49 sequences of recorded video and 63,215 face images were gathered from the internet (VGG FACE). It contains 244X244 size of the input image and the 227 class, which is the image's output. The dimensionality of the fully connected layer is 4098. The xi is of N X N-dimensional image. m is the size of a convolutional neural network. Functions that are non-linear are denoted by σ. Yij represents the output of the convolution.

EXPERIMENTAL RESULTS

The number of individuals captured in the video frames is shown in Fig. (**1**). A total of 5 people entered through the video recorder, which was managed to capture 126 recorded video frames. Each individual is photographed in five different poses. Such frames have been pre-processed and then sent to the scheme of the viola jones method which further retrieves facial segments from them. Feature extraction was then carried out using reinforcement learning. Fig. (**4**) represents the fetched facial subject, as well as HOG feature visualization, a plot of histogram feature points, as well as a correlation between recorded video frames having the same type of person [10].

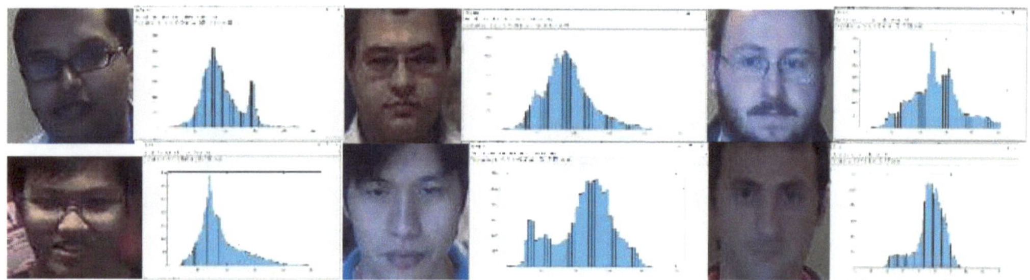

Fig (4). Facial features in histogram representation.

The above figure shows the representation of facial features in histogram representation. The model clearly indicates that each individual has been described uniquely with the help of histogram representation. Hence, the model is able to identify each individual from frames that contain the crowd capture. These histogram features are utilized for training purposes.

Fig. (**5**) shows the sample of captured facial subjects from video surveillance. A rectangular block has been plotted around the facial content by the Viola Jones algorithm based on the feature plot (green dots). Fig. (**6**) shows samples of images with localized facial features that depict the ROC curve, which depicts the model's overall accuracy performance.

The proposed model indicated an average accuracy to be 98.85% for all the dataset video frames. The minimum error rate is also shown in the lower part of Fig. (**6**). The figure depicts an ROC (Receiver Operating Characteristic) curve, which is used to visualize the recognition rate or performance of the model. The ROC curve showcases the relationship between the true positive rate (sensitivity) and the false positive rate (1 - specificity) at various classification thresholds.

Fig. (5). Samples of images with localized facial features.

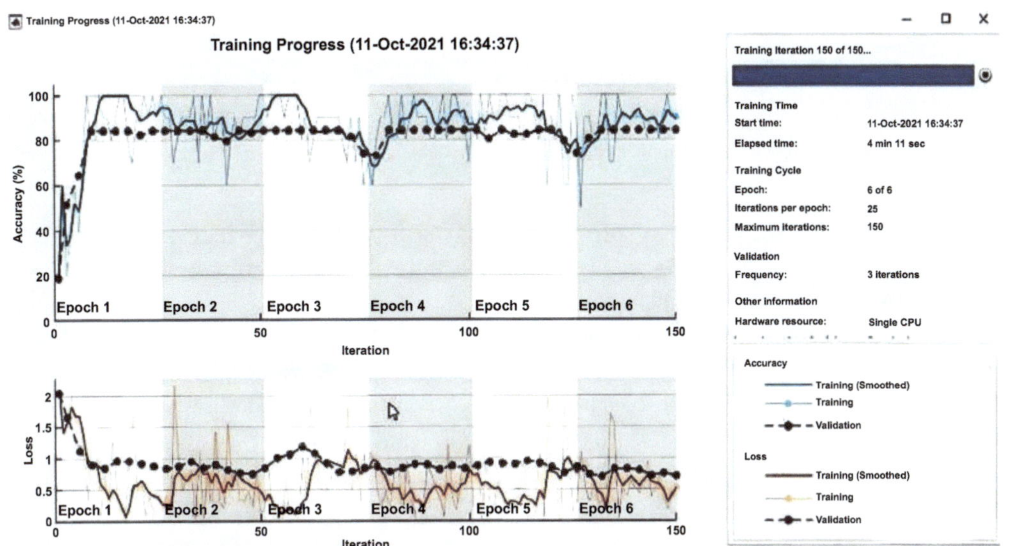

Fig. (6). ROC curve to depict recognition rate of model.

By analyzing the ROC curve, one can gain insights into the model's ability to distinguish between different classes or categories. The curve's shape and distance from the diagonal line (which represents random guessing) provide information about the model's effectiveness. A curve closer to the top-left corner indicates higher recognition rates, while a curve closer to the diagonal line signifies lower performance.

Fig. (7) shows the confusion matrix evaluated for the set of samples of video data containing 6 numbers of people. It is clear from the above figure that the algorithm has a high average accuracy for the recognition of the video dataset containing unprecedented noise affects.

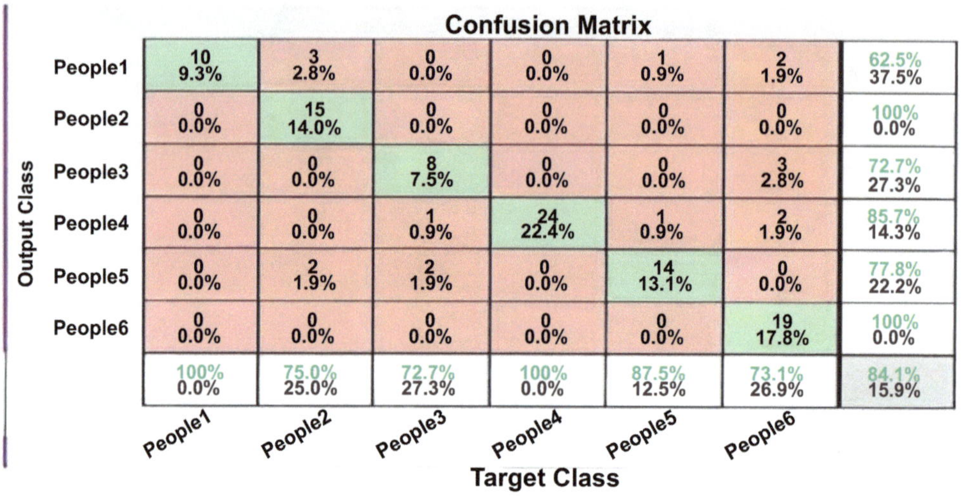

Confusion Matrix

Output Class \ Target Class	People1	People2	People3	People4	People5	People6	
People1	10 9.3%	3 2.8%	0 0.0%	0 0.0%	1 0.9%	2 1.9%	62.5% 37.5%
People2	0 0.0%	15 14.0%	0 0.0%	0 0.0%	0 0.0%	0 0.0%	100% 0.0%
People3	0 0.0%	0 0.0%	8 7.5%	0 0.0%	0 0.0%	3 2.8%	72.7% 27.3%
People4	0 0.0%	0 0.0%	1 0.9%	24 22.4%	1 0.9%	2 1.9%	85.7% 14.3%
People5	0 0.0%	2 1.9%	2 1.9%	0 0.0%	14 13.1%	0 0.0%	77.8% 22.2%
People6	0 0.0%	0 0.0%	0 0.0%	0 0.0%	0 0.0%	19 17.8%	100% 0.0%
	100% 0.0%	75.0% 25.0%	72.7% 27.3%	100% 0.0%	87.5% 12.5%	73.1% 26.9%	84.1% 15.9%

Fig. (7). Confusion matrix of the proposed scheme.

Table **1** shows the proposed system in comparison with recent technologies.

Table 1. Recent publications are compared.

S. No.	Techniques	Accuracy/Result
1.	A scheme of Neural Network accompanied by Rough Contour and Estimation Routine [5]	The rate of recognition is 92.1 percent.
2.	Using Eigen faces in PCA [6]	It was able to achieve an accuracy rate of 83%.
3.	PCA-based local Gabor Filter followed by LDA [7]	With the help of PCA and LDA features, a recognition rate of 97.33% was determined.
4.	A method based on 2D appearance and the Radial Symmetry Transform [8].	Face expressions of happiness and surprise were given an 83% rating. And for angry and sad expressions, 78 % Accuracy is required.
5.	Support Vector Machine and 2D-LDA [9]	The rate of recognition is 95.71%.
6.	Proposed Scheme	The rate of recognition is 98.85%.

CONCLUSION

The effective and fast technique for face recognition from video input is described in this proposed methodology. To accomplish this task, the experiment uses the Viola Jones algorithm, the deep reinforcement learning method, as well as the rest net 101 architecture. The highest recognition accuracy is attained up-to 98.85% for 100 samples of images taken in real-time. The extracted images are also subjected to a variety of image processing attacks to see if the model can recognize the attacked images. And the results are found to be satisfied. Further analysis of attacked images in various aspects is part of future work. The model is also recognizing multiple faces when captured together in one video frame.

REFERENCES

[1] M. Turk, and A. Pentland, "Eigenfaces for recognition", *J. Cogn. Neurosci.,* vol. 3, no. 1, pp. 71-86, 1991.
[http://dx.doi.org/10.1162/jocn.1991.3.1.71] [PMID: 23964806]

[2] Y. Hu, A.S. Mian, and R. Owens, Sparse approximated nearest points for image set classification. *CVPR.* 2011 USA, pp. 121-128.
[http://dx.doi.org/10.1109/CVPR.2011.5995500]

[3] Z. Huang, and L Van Gool, "A riemannian network for spd matrix learning", *arXiv:1608.04233.*

[4] S.S. Kshatri, and D. Singh, "Convolutional neural network in medical image analysis: A review", *Arch. Comput. Methods Eng.,* vol. 30, no. 4, pp. 2793-2810, 2023.
[http://dx.doi.org/10.1007/s11831-023-09898-w]

[5] Available from: http://arma.sourceforge.net/chokepoint/

[6] Z. Cao, Q. Yin, X. Tang, and J. Sun, Face recognition with learning- based descriptor.*CVPR.* IEEE, 2010, pp. 2707-2714.

[7] Z. Lei, M. Pietikäinen, and S.Z. Li, "Learning discriminant face descriptor", *IEEE Trans. Pattern Anal. Mach. Intell.,* vol. 36, no. 2, pp. 289-302, 2014.
[http://dx.doi.org/10.1109/TPAMI.2013.112] [PMID: 24356350]

[8] S.S. Kshatri, S. Sharma, and G.R. Sinha, *An investigation of the coronavirus disease (COVID-19).* Mortality Risk Using Machine Learning, 2022, pp. 1-24.
[http://dx.doi.org/10.4018/978-1-7998-9831-3.ch001]

[9] W. Deng, J. Hu, J. Guo, H. Zhang, and C. Zhang, "Comments on "globally maximizing, locally minimizing: Unsupervised discriminant projection with application to face and palm biometrics", *EEE Trans. Pattern Anal. Mach. Intell.,* vol. 30, no. 8, pp. 1503-1504, 2008.
[http://dx.doi.org/10.1109/TPAMI.2007.70783] [PMID: 18566503]

[10] X. He, S. Yan, Y. Hu, P. Niyogi, and H.J. Zhang, "Face recognition using Laplacianfaces", *IEEE Trans. Pattern Anal. Mach. Intell.,* vol. 27, no. 3, pp. 328-340, 2005.
[http://dx.doi.org/10.1109/TPAMI.2005.55] [PMID: 15747789]

CHAPTER 6

Multimedia Security in Audio Signal

Ritesh Diwaker[1,*] and **Deepak Asrani**[1]

[1] *Department of Computer Science and Engineering, BN College of Engineering and Technology, Lucknow, India*

Abstract: The security of Digital media has been varying continuously due to advanced malware attacks. Multimedia security has become one of the major concerns since new technologies are introduced. The proposed paper applied the watermarking technique in digital audio signals in which unique data is inserted in one-dimensional data in such a way that it must not affect the major information of the audio signal. The hybrid decomposition scheme has been applied to the audio data in order to extract features in terms of energy bands. The data is kept hidden in a low significant energy band that contains less information. This watermarking technique ensures the ownership of the multimedia data. Only authorized authors can be able to claim ownership of the audio data. The correct authorization of audio data can be proven by the extraction method in which the hidden watermark data has been extracted back to its original form without leaving any distortion in audio data. The proposed work introduces a hybrid approach to watermarking 2D data into an audio file. A hybrid audio decomposition technique was introduced by the proposed scheme in which a dual form of audio decomposition method has been applied containing Fast Fourier transform (FFT) and Cordic QR scheme. The correct location from the energy band has been found to embed the watermark data. Before the embedding procedure, the watermarking data has been selected. The proposed method selects an image containing information as a watermark that is first encrypted before initiating the embedding process. Watermark Encryption has been done using a cyclic coding algorithm and Arnold's cat map. The disintegration of the audio file will finally result in Q and R matrices. Both such matrices are of orthogonal type. Then, the encrypted watermark data has been implanted in a random fashion in the R component of decomposed audio data during the embedding process. The inverse procedure has been applied for the watermark extraction and decryption process.

Keywords: Fast fourier transformation, Q-R cordic decomposition, Watermarking in audio signals, Watermark encryption, Watermark embedding, Water- mark extraction.

* **Corresponding author Ritesh Diwaker:** Department of Computer Science and Engineering, BN College of Engineering and Technology, Lucknow, India; E-mail: riteshdiwakar12@gmail.com

Suman Kumar Swarnkar, Sapna Singh Kshatri, Virendra Kumar Swarnkar & Tien Anh Tran (Eds.)

INTRODUCTION

Multimedia security is one of the challenging concepts in research field. Securing multimedia using encryption is found to be the most frequently used technique. Various encryption techniques [1] have been utilized earlier but few challenges remain untouched. The basic challenge is to tackle advanced hacking algorithms [2] that generally varies according to an algorithm. A cyber attacker is used to exploit the vulnerability of the existing system and uses hacking algorithm to obtain unauthorized access. When it comes to digital rights management, the watermarking [3] method is one of the reliable techniques applied to secure multimedia content by hiding watermark data in the host multimedia data. The challenging concept in the watermarking approach is to maintain balance among imperceptibility, robustness, and payload. The watermarked audio signal must be imperceptible so that no watermark hidden clue can be generated in terms of noise. The robustness has been measured under the application of signal-processing attacks. The influence of the hidden watermark has been seen under the application of attacks in multimedia signals. Payload is the amount of the data that will be inserted into the host multimedia. Therefore, the maximum payload must be kept in order to maintain digital right management while maintaining imperceptibility and robustness. Various existing approaches [4] fail to establish a balance among these three factors and therefore may leave a loophole for the imposter.

RELATED WORK

A model based on a human interface system contains an input sensor to employ facial expressions, an ECG signal reader, a voice recorder, a body movement video recorder, etc. The interface records the body signals to extract feature variation that can be used for watermark hiding. Liscombe *et al.* [5] performed feature extraction from non-static speech one-dimensional input signal containing amplitude, pitch, frequency variation, etc. In the past years [6], various algorithms were developed to recognize human feelings. Researches include algorithms such as support vector machine, Gaussian mixture models, hidden Markov models, etc. in order to find suitable energy bands for the embedding process. A multimodal [7] system for the watermarking of image data into facial expression signals is used, in which two different body signals are employed over a single deep learning algorithm for better embedding. Pan *et al.* [8] studied a hybrid fusion of a multimodal system by using visual and textual signals from an individual for the watermarking approach. The model uses an LSTM algorithm for feature extraction from both datasets. Siriwardhana *et al.* [6] implemented a self-supervised learning model for the textural input data from people to embed the data by applying modalities in the feature vector. Priyasad *et al.* [7] introduced a deep learning scheme for the analysis of features such as acoustic features by applying the band pass filtering technique. The features are represented in the N-gram level in a bidirectional recurrent network. Krishna *et al.* [8] utilized a raw waveform dataset over a neural network algorithm. They applied audio processing in order to refine the feature vector to obtain the enhanced energy spectrum for the insertion of the watermark so that the data must be hidden in good format. Lee *et al.* [9] applied a deep learning algorithm that uses a multimodal system containing textual details and facial images in order to find a correlation between the embedding and extraction process. Liu *et al.* [10] used an LSTM network for the recognition of emotions from audio features. The method was also tested with a machine learning algorithm for feature analysis. LSTM modal describes the interpretation of lyrics from audio signals and correlates the meaning variation of noises for the detection of any hidden entity in the host signal. Most strategies in earlier literature [11] were based on facial expression correlation watermarking hiding technique. The facial image dataset contains a 2-dimensional representation of Gabor wavelet for the extraction of characteristics. Table **1** shows the literature that presents various strategies for emotion recognition. Each study focuses on different modalities, techniques, datasets, and feature vectors for accurate emotion classification. The accuracy obtained in each study is reported as the average accuracy achieved based on their respective experiments and evaluations.

Table 1. Few recent literature containing various emotion recognition strategies.

Reference	Modal	Technique	Dataset	Feature vector	Accuracy Obtained
Jayalaxmi J *et al.* [3]	SVM, KNN	Blind water-marking	JAFFE	LBP, DTC, Viola Jones face detection	91.85% average accuracy
Li W *et al.* [4]	CNN	Hybrid feature decomposition	CIFE dataset	Filter, transforms and viola jones face detector	82.4% average accuracy
Mehendale N. et al. [5]	Deep Learning	Spatial do- main	CMU, NIST dataset	Skin tone detection	85% average accuracy
Islam B. *et al.* [6]	ANN	Frequency Domain	JAFFE	HOG, LBP, Viola Jones	93.51% average accuracy
Singh G *et al.* [8]	ROI based FER	Hybrid de-composition	JAFFE	Audio features	75% average accuracy

In earlier work, it has been seen that most of the watermarking tasks are based on static images. The challenging task in the earlier work is to maintain the balance among the payload, robustness, and imperceptibility. A hidden watermark must contain enough information in order to secure ownership of the host data [12].

The proposed paper utilizes an R component matrix generated by QR decomposition and obtained diagonal elements which are found to be stable and leave no distortion in the relevant information of audio data. The encrypted watermark data has been implanted in a random way which means that the exact location of the embedding process is not specific [13]. The location of the embedding process has been decided by a pseudo-random sequence generated by a pseudo-random key used by the proposed scheme. The extraction process contains just the reverse procedure of the embedding process in which the watermarked audio data first undergone into the inverse of QR and FFT hybrid decomposition in order to extract R matrix in which the watermarked data is hidden. Then, the same pseudo random sequence key has been used to extract the hidden encryption watermark bits from the audio data. The extracted watermark bits are then decrypted using inverse of Arnold's cat and cyclic coding in order to identify the exact watermark image data.

The chapter scheme of the proposed work is given as follows: The proposed methodology has been given in section II. The experimental results are illustrated in section III. The conclusion part of this work is given in section IV. Section V will discuss the reference used in the proposed paper.

PROPOSED METHODOLOGY

The proposed methodology enrols watermarking techniques over dataset containing an audio signal of 45.1 kHz sampling rate. The proposed methodology also takes a watermark (a logo) as an image of the size 16 (Height) by 16 (Width). A sample of audio signal and a watermark image is shown in Fig. (**1**).

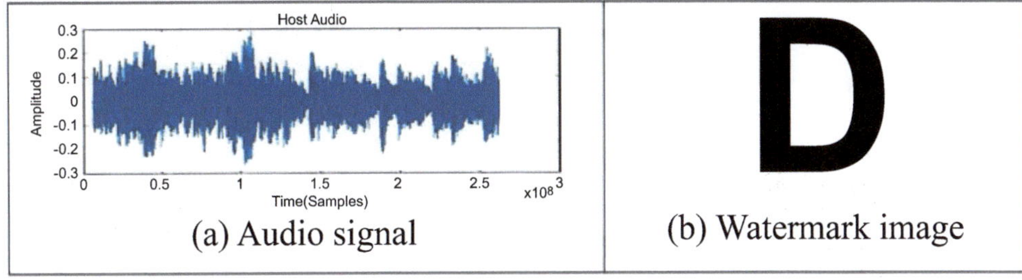

Fig. (1). Sample host and watermark data.

The audio dataset has been taken from a standard dataset named SAMAINE [4] which contains audio signals of standard music signals including Jazz, Blues, and Pop. Fig. (**1b**) shows a sample of a watermark image of payload 256 bits which is selected to embed into an audio signal.

Fig. (**2**) describes the procedure of an audio watermark.

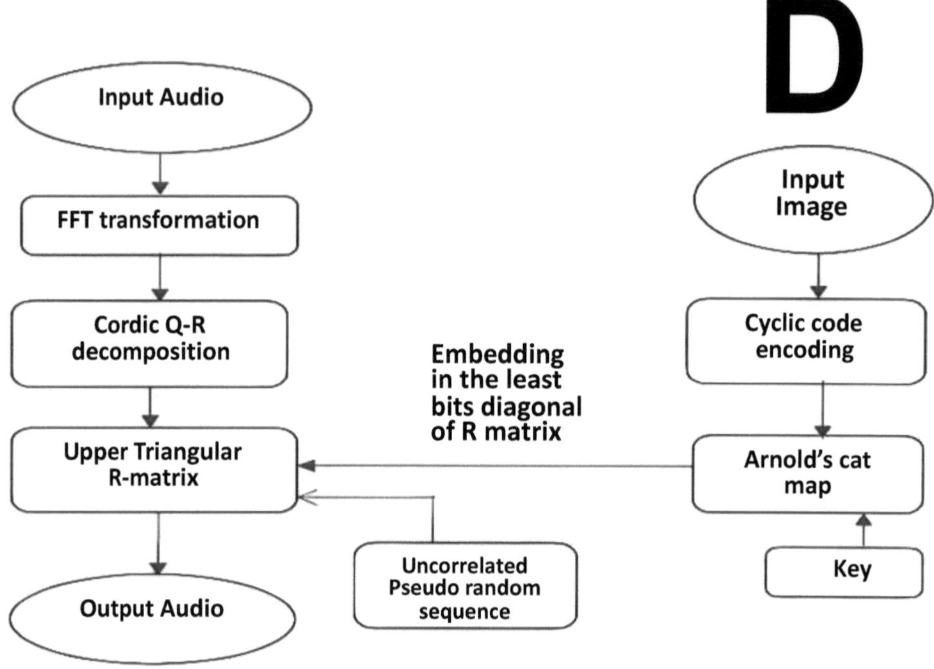

Fig. (2). Procedure of audio watermarking.

Fig. (**2**) of the proposed embedding technique demonstrates decomposition of the audio signal into fixed-sized frequency components using the Fast Fourier Transform (FFT) method. This technique divides the audio signal into distinct frequency bands containing specific audio information. Significantly, the frequency bands do not overlap, allowing for separate analysis and processing of the audio signal in different frequency ranges.

The watermark image as shown in Fig. (**1b**) has been encrypted first using a cyclic encoding technique [4] in which encrypted watermark bits are generated with the multiplication of data bits (watermark itself) and the generator polynomial. Further, Arnold's cat [5] map has been applied to scramble the encoded watermark bits to ensure dual security.

FFT Decomposition of Audio Signal

In the embedding process, first, the FFT decomposition is applied to the host audio signal. Equations of FFT transformation are given below.

$$e^{-j2\pi ap/n} = -j\sin\left(\frac{2\pi ap}{n}\right) + \cos\left(2\pi ap/n\right) \quad (1)$$

Equation 1 shows the F[a] that is used to generate frequency component of the audio signal containing the intensity of pixel information.

QR-Cordic Decomposition

Cordic QR decomposition is applied onto the selected frequency components in order to generate most stable energy band for the watermark embedding purpose. Givens transformation has been used inside this decomposition to find Q and R orthogonal matrices. Watermark hiding has been done in the least bits of the upper triangular R orthogonal matrix which is found to be stable and create minimal distortion to the host signal.

Watermark Embedding Technique

A watermark image (logo) first underwent encryption by applying 7×4 cyclic encoding technique. In this technique, watermark bits are dissolved into 4-bit groups which are multiplied with the generation polynomial to generate 7 encoded bits containing 3 redundant bits. After getting encoding watermark bits, the proposed model applied Arnold's cat map technique in order to scramble the encrypted 2- 2-dimensional encoding watermark. In Arnold's cat map technique, the value of key has been taken as 7 which means that the scrambling of the encrypted watermark has been done with the fixed rate for 7 times. This will ensure dual layer security of the watermark. After, the watermark data are inserted by replacing the last bits of the diagonal of the R matrix of the host audio signal. Insertion of watermark has been made with the help of pseudo-random sequence in which replacement has been done in the random places of the host audio signal so that it cannot be easily detected or removed by any attacker. A pseudo-random technique presents a mathematical approach to generate random places in the host audio signal in which watermark bits can be placed. The aim of the proposed model is to maintain a perfect balance between imperceptibility, robustness and payload. After the generation of a watermarked audio, the analysis of watermarked audio has been made by using PSNR ratios in order to calculate any kind of distortion. Fig. (**3**) shows the watermark extraction process.

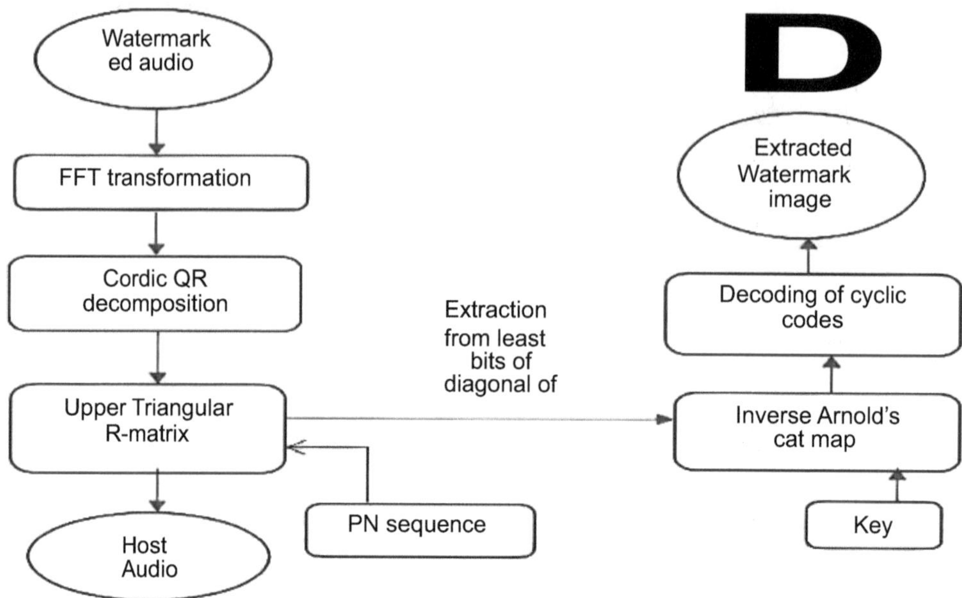

Fig. (3). Procedure of extrication of watermark data.

In Fig. (**3**), the PSNR value is found to be 37.76 dB approx. in case of audio signal containing hidden watermark. The PSNR, BER and NC in case of rescued watermark data is also given as 66.02%, 0.10% and 0.89%, respectively.

The watermark extrication procedure has been depicted in Fig. (**2**) in which the watermark data containing audio (watermarked audio) has undergone disintegration with Fast Fourier and QR decomposition to obtain an upper triangular R matrix. Then, the same pseudo-random sequence is applied for the extrication of hidden watermark bits. The extricated watermark data are then descrambled using the same inverse Arnold's cat map algorithm 7 times. Further, the inverse of cyclic coding is applied to decode the actual watermark bits by removing the influence of generation polynomial and redundant bits. After the extraction of watermark bits, the analysis of the watermark image is done using normalized cross-correlation, bit error rate, and PSNR ratios.

EXPERIMENTAL RESULTS

A two-dimensional reshaped host audio signal of size 512×512 has been used in the procedure of watermark embedding. Then 16×16 watermark image has been inserted into the host audio. Three types of audio signals have been taken in this experiment including Blues, Pop and Classic. Figure below depicts the graphical user interface containing audio watermarking analysis.

Fig. (**4**) depicts the proposed model's graphical user interface (GUI). The GUI is the visual interface allowing users to interact with the model and perform various tasks. It presents a user-friendly layout and design, showcasing different elements such as buttons, menus, input fields, and output displays.

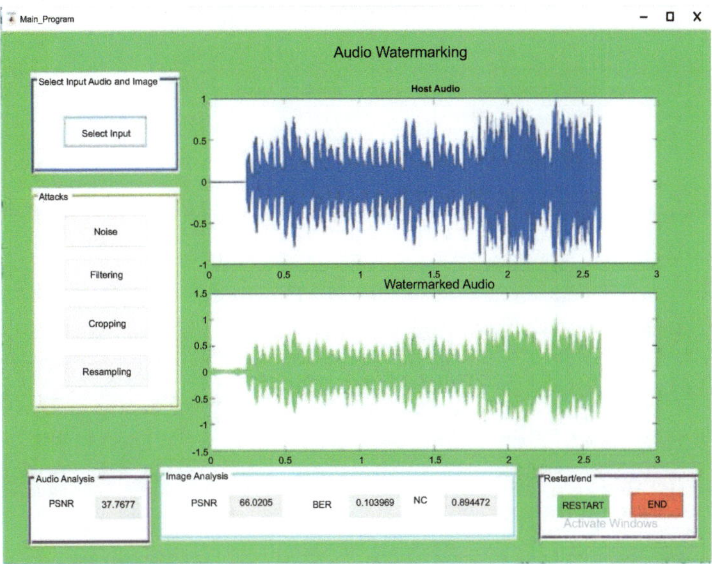

Fig. (4). GUI of the proposed model.

The GUI provides a convenient way for users to input data, adjust model parameters, initiate processes, and view the results or feedback generated by the model. It enhances the overall usability and accessibility of the proposed model, making it easier for users to interact with and utilize its functionalities. Distortion-less qualifying criteria of watermarked audio is more than 20dB but it must not exceed more than 60dB. For the image, the PSNR value and NC value should be more with no boundary condition. But the bit error rate (BER) must be as low as possible. A result sample of a watermark (before the embedding) and the rescued watermark (after the extraction) has been depicted in Fig. (**4**).

Fig. (**5**) visually demonstrates that the extracted watermark image after the extraction process has minimal distortion traces. The picture shows that the extracted watermark remains intact and recognizable, with few visible distortions or artifacts. This indicates the effectiveness of the extraction process in accurately retrieving the watermark from the watermarked image.

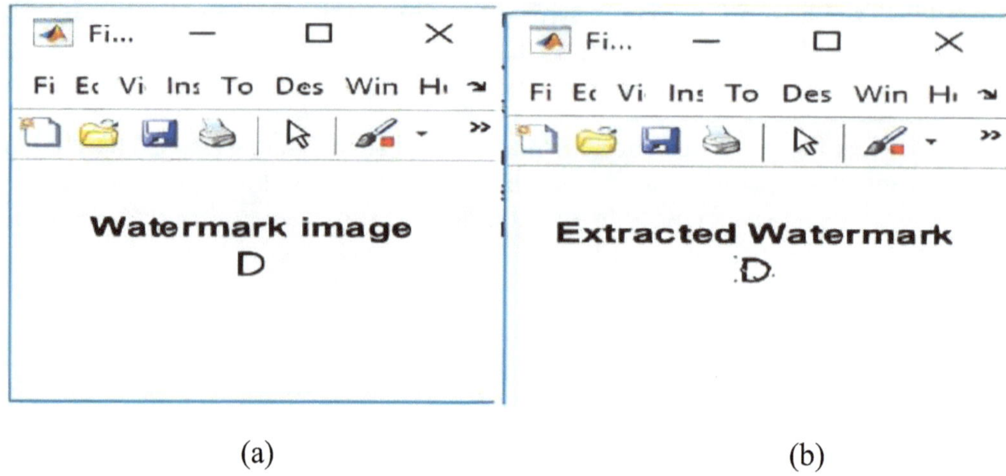

(a) (b)

Fig. (5). (**a**) Watermark (Before the embedding) (**b**) Extricated watermark (After the embedding).

The high fidelity of the extracted watermark suggests that the proposed method successfully preserves the integrity and quality of the watermark during the extraction process. Therefore, the proposed model is able to rescue the watermark bits safely, from audio, with the very least distortion so that the ownership can be easily claimed in the digital right management policy [7]. The result analysis of host data and watermark data is mentioned in Table **2** for all types of audio signals *i.e.*, Blues, Pop, and Classic.

Table 2. Analysis of watermarked audio and extracted watermark image.

Quality Assessment of Watermarked Audio		**Quality Assessment of Extracted Watermark Image**		
Type of Au- dio	PSNR Value (dB)	Bit Error Rate	Normal- ized Cross Correlation	PSNR-Value (dB)
Blues Type	36.64	0.03	0.89	65.03
Classic Type	34.65	0.05	0.91	63.62
Pop Type	37.53	0.06	0.93	55.15

The quality assessment of extracted extricated watermark has also been tested under the application of various attacks such as filtering, resampling and noise attack.

Fig. (**6**) shows the influence of noise, filtering and resampling of extracted watermark images.

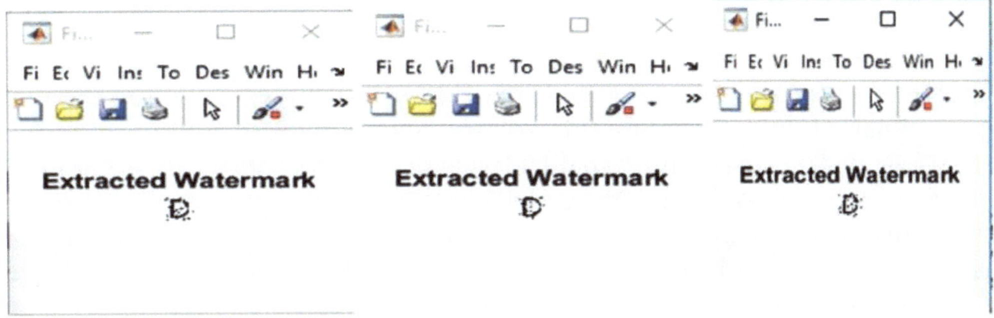

Fig. (6). Extracted watermark image analysis after applying attacks. (**a**) Influence of noise (**b**) influence of Filtering (**c**) influence of resampling.

Fig. (**5**) gives the rescued (extricated from attacked watermarked audio signal) watermark images that are presented under the influence of various attacks. Some distortion traces have been seen in the image. However the image information after the attacks is enough to prove the ownership. The proposed model achieved the net value of Normalized cross-correlation and a Bit error rate of 93.5% and 0.65%, respectively. Hence, the proposed model is found to be robust against attacks.

From Table **3**, it is evident that the proposed model is able to secure robust and is able to secure watermark image after the implication of various image processing attacks.

Table 3. Extracted watermark analysis under the implication of attacks.

Types of audios and attacks applied		**Quality Assessment of Ex- tracted Watermark Image under the influence of attacks**	
Types of Audios	Types of Attacks	BER rate	NC value
Blues Types	Noise attack	0.45	0.87
	Audio Filtering	0.23	0.83
	Resampling the rate	0.22	0.92
Classic Types	Noise attack	0.42	0.91
	Audio Filtering	0.33	0.90
	Resampling the rate	0.21	0.88
Pop Types	Noise attack	0.26	0.90
	Audio Filtering	0.56	0.87
	Resampling the rate	0.62	0.90

CONCLUSION

The proposed model performed watermarking in digital audio signal to secure the multimedia ownership. A watermark image has been successfully inserted in the audio signal while maintaining the balance among imperceptibility, robustness and pay load. The host audio signal has been decomposed under FFT and Cordic QR decomposition to obtain energy band for hiding the watermark. Before the embedding, a two-layer encryption technique *i.e.* cyclic coding and Arnold's cat map has been applied. The Pseudo random sequence has been used for the insertion of watermark into host audio signal successfully. The watermarked host has been analyzed for distortion. The average value of peak signal to noise ratio of the audio signal (consisting of watermark bits) is found to be 37.8 dB which ensures the correctness of the model. The extraction process has been done with the inverse of the same procedure that is followed during the embedding process. The extracted watermark image has been analyzed using a bit error rate and normalized cross correlation matrices. The results are found to be satisfying enough to recognize watermark information.

REFERENCES

[1] M.A. Akhaee, M.J. Saberian, S. Feizi, and F. Marvasti, "Method based obscuring data in audio signal using correlated quantization followed by histogram-based detector", *IEEE Trans. Multimed.,* vol. 11, no. 5, pp. 834-842, 2009. [http://dx.doi.org/10.1109/TMM.2009.2012923]

[2] H. Ozer, B. Sankur, and N. Memon, "An audio watermarking structure using SVD disinte- gration technique", *Proc. Seventh ACM workshop on multimedia and data privacy.* 2005, pp.51-56 .

[3] V.K. Bhat, I. Sengupta, and A. Das, "A robust method uses singular value decomposition for an adaptive audio watermarking system in wavelet domain", *Digit. Signal Process.,* vol. 20, no. 6, pp. 1547-1558, 2010. [http://dx.doi.org/10.1016/j.dsp.2010.02.006]

[4] P. Hu, D. Peng, Z. Yi, and Y. Xiang, "Robust time-spread echo watermarking using characteristics of host signals", *Electron. Lett.,* vol. 52, no. 1, pp. 5-6, 2016. [http://dx.doi.org/10.1049/el.2015.1508]

[5] HT Hu, LY Hsu, and HH Chou, *Perceptual-based DWPT-DCT framework for selective blind audio watermarking.,* vol. 105, pp. 316-627, 2014.*Signal Process,* vol. 105, pp. 316-627, 2014. [http://dx.doi.org/10.1016/j.sigpro.2014.05.003]

[6] B. Sharma, and M. Dave, "Robust hybrid image and audio watermarking using cyclic codes and arnold transform", *2019 International Conference on Communication and Electronics Systems (ICCES)* 17-19 July 2019, Coimbatore, India, pp. 309-315 . [http://dx.doi.org/10.1109/ICCES45898.2019.9002117]

[7] P.K. Dhar, and I. Echizen, "Robust FFT Based Watermarking Scheme for Copyright Pro- tection of Digital Audio Data", *7th International Conference on Intelligent Information Hiding and Multimedia Signal Processing* 2011, Dalian, pp.181-184 .

[8] H. Karajeh, "proposed a watermarking system relied on dual decomposition using DWT and Schur technique, published in spinger science", *Multimedia Tools Appl.,* vol. 78, pp. pages18395-18418, 2019. [http://dx.doi.org/10.1007/s11042-019-7214-3]

[9] H. Subir, and A.M. Joshi, "DWT-DCT based blind audio watermarking using Arnold scram- bling and Cyclic codes", *International Conference on Signal Processing and Integrated Networks (SPIN-2019)* 07-08 March 2019, Noida, pp.79-84.

[10] K. Chen, F. Yan, and A.M. Iliyasu, "Watermarking system using dual quantum audio procedure relied on quantum discrete cosine transform", *Int. J. Theor. Phys.,* vol. 58, pp. 502-521, 2019. [http://dx.doi.org/10.1007/s10773-018-3950-9]

[11] A.K Dwivedi, M.K. Dutta, R. Burget, and V. Myska, "An efficient and robust zero-bit watermarking technique for biometric image protection", *International Confer- ence on Signal Processing,,* Budapest, Hungary, pp. 236-240, 2019.

[12] K. Vivekananda Bhat, A.K. Das, and J.H. Lee, "A mean quantization watermarking scheme for audio signals using singular-value decomposition", *IEEE Access,* vol. 7, pp. 157480-157488, 2019. [http://dx.doi.org/10.1109/ACCESS.2019.2949691]

[13] A.K Gupta, M.K. Dutta, and J. Schimmel, "Perceptually transparent & robust audio watermarking algorithm using multi resolution decomposition & cordic QR decomposition", *International Conference on Signal Processing (TSP)* 2019, Budapest, Hungary pp.313-317.

CHAPTER 7

Recent Advancements and Impact of Multimedia in Education

Gausiya Yasmeen[1], **Syed Adnan Afaq**[1,*], **Mohd Faisal**[1] and **Saman Uzma**[2]

[1] *Department of Computer Application, Integral University, Lucknow, India*

[2] *Cubeight Solutions Sydney, Sydney, Australia*

Abstract: The term "multimedia learning" refers to education that combines words and images. Reading a physics textbook, seeing a recorded lecture, or watching a PowerPoint presentation are all examples of multimedia learning. Also with the advent of artificial intelligence, the format of the learning procedure has now become more advanced, personalized, and relevant as students can get their answers more random with full specification as compared to earlier processes. The 21st century, known colloquially as the era of information and technology (IT), is currently in effect. Nowadays, the educational sector makes extensive use of information and technology to make teaching and learning successful and enjoyable for both teachers and students. Teachers are the cornerstone of any society that is able to function. The use of technology is crucial in teacher training programmers. Students can learn and gain information through varied sources like the Internet, digital media, cable networks, and social media sites like Whatsapp, Linkedin, Igo, Line, Facebook, Twitter, and Wechat. Thus, multimedia, Information, and Communication Technologies (ICT) play a significant role in training purposes and enhancing skills of teaching abilities. In the ushering era of technology, namely multimedia, it is now utilized as a teaching tool. Multimedia applications can be designed in effective ways to produce successful educational results, according to several researchers and educators. Not only that, but we'll also talk about the definition of multimedia, how it relates to learning tools, the idea of multimedia applications, how they're made using various media, the kinds of educational components that encourage students to learn in their natural environments, and real-world problems. This article explains the concepts and traits of multimedia and educational components. In light of the many altering needs of our society, attention is now paid to various educational conceptions and practices. Changes are being made in teacher education as well, as per these beliefs and practices. The interdisciplinary approach, correspondence courses, orientation courses, and other modern trends in teacher education are included below. Other methods utilized in teacher education include team teaching, programmed instruction, micro-teaching, and simulations. Action research is now used in teacher education as well.

* **Corresponding author Syed Adnan Afaq:** Department of Computer Application, Integral University, Lucknow, India; E-mail: saafaq@iul.ac.in

Suman Kumar Swarnkar, Sapna Singh Kshatri, Virendra Kumar Swarnkar & Tien Anh Tran (Eds.)

Keywords: Educational, ICT, Information and Technology, Multimedia, Simulations, Technology, Teacher Training.

INTRODUCTION

An educational scenario where a pupil has the power to study the module at one's own place and in accordance with one's own preferences, needs, and thought abilities where interactive multimedia for instruction is most commonly used. The major purpose of collaborative multimedia study material is to completely alter the role of the instructor rather than to completely exchange the educator. As a result, multimedia ought to be exceptionally well-designed and clever enough to replicate the best educator by integrating the best design techniques with the numerous components of cognitive processes. In the sphere of education, we support classroom instruction *via* audio, video, slides, overhead transparencies, *etc*. A mixture of many media is referred to as multimedia. People began utilizing computers to accomplish numerous jobs to ease their lives as they became commonplace in society. A trustworthy technical advancement, interactive multimedia has the ability to update how we read and discover new information. Information and Communication Technology (ICT) is a key component of modern life in practically every aspect. The use of ICT technologies in the social and academic spheres has altered the social and academic environment as a whole. All schools, colleges, and institutions remain closed due to lockdown during the COVID-19 epidemic [1]. This has an impact on student academic loss. In order to counter this, ICT technologies are utilized to stop academic loss among students, keep in touch with them, keep them engaged, offer them tasks, and get their feedback. Information and communication technology (ICT) has steadily raised the bar for education, affecting instructional strategies, learning techniques, scientific inquiry, and information availability. Information and communication technology (ICT) emphasizes the role of an intelligent building management system by integrating telecom, computers, the internet, tools, middleware, storage, wireless communications, phone, text messaging, video and audio, networking sites (Face book), voice over Internet protocol (VoIP), as well as other communication mediums [2]. All aspects of digital data storage, retrieval, modification, transmission, and receipt are covered. It has slowly evolved from an educational society to a knowledge and information society, transforming the economy into a knowledge economy and assisting countries in developing their ability for knowledge-based wealth creation. It is a leading-edge high-tech method that will have a huge impact on the educational system.

The obligation to educate children falls on every country. It is a fundamental right of theirs. However, it also refers to the right to get great education from a qualified teacher, not only the right to access education. Education has a long history of being associated with social responsibility and societal empowerment procedure. However, the era of globalization, is evolving around a socio-commercial pursuit that arose uniquely endowing society a combination of traditional and contemporary approaches. Technical know-how has become the foundation of every single thing in today's hypercompetitive realm. Also, AI (Artificial Intelligence) has empowered education and education techniques like Examination Integrity, Plagiarism Detection Chatbots for enrollment and retention, LMSs, faculty lecture transcription, improved online discussion boards, student success metrics analysis, and academic research [3]. AI is boosting personalized learning plans and educational tracks for students, encouraging tutoring by assisting students in honing their strengths and strengthening their weak areas, facilitating rapid interaction between teachers and students, and promoting universal 24/7 learning access. AI enables teachers to provide pupils with individualized responses to pertinent queries. In accordance with the problems and inquiries they encounter in course materials and online sessions, it also aids in students' education. Students can now communicate with teachers *via* a more extensive mechanism. The Learning Management System (LMS) enables educators to develop courses, deliver instruction, facilitate communication, and student participation in collaborative effort, appraise educational outcomes, and provide added resources for students' assistance, thereby assisting schools in maintaining the integrity of their educational programs [4]. You may consolidate all of your training materials, resources, personal development goals, assessment results, and progress outcomes using an LMS. This has made things effortlessly easy to check which activities are accomplished and by whom. Also, the identification of content was made effective, provided with continuous training. Nearly all universities nowadays assert to have a plan in place to make use of the potential offered by the internet or other digital media in order to enhance and develop conventional education. In the middle of the 1990s, when the World Wide Web first appeared, the phrase "e-learning" was invented, creating buzz. Some predicted sweeping changes to the educational landscape or the demise of conventional education as a whole. In the paper, we will discuss how multimedia and various technologies have changed the traditional face of imparting quality education.

MULTIMEDIA

The presentation of text, images, music, and video together with links and other tools that enable the user to explore, connect, create, and converse using a computer is known as multimedia. The concept provided above includes four elements that are crucial to multimedia. They are:

• A device that you may use to interact and coordinate your hearing and vision.

• Binding of the information through links.

• Tools for navigating the network of interconnected information.

• Methods for you to collect, process, and share your own thoughts.

Fig. (**1**) depicts the multimedia concept, highlighting the four essential elements contributing to its existence. The elements include text, graphics, audios, and videos, and the figure illustrates that the absence of any of these elements would result in a lack of multimedia.

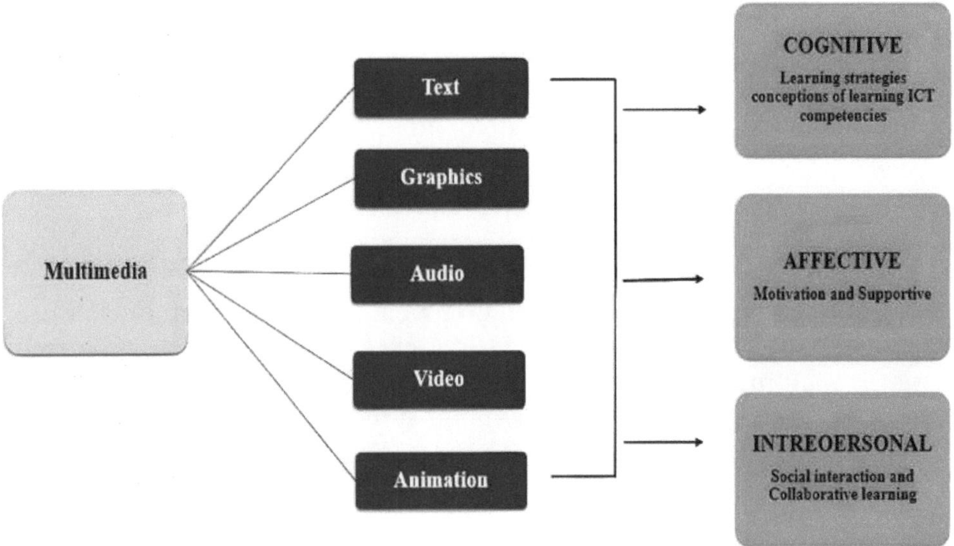

Fig. (1). Concept of multimedia.

The concept emphasizes that an ideal multimedia project effectively integrates all four elements, utilizing them in a cohesive and complementary manner. Combined, these elements enhance the overall user experience by providing a rich and interactive multimedia presentation.

The figure also indicates that the term "multimedia" is relatively recent in its field, suggesting that integrating various media elements to create a multimedia experience has gained significant attention and recognition recently.

There will be a lack of multimedia if any one of these elements is absent. An ideal multimedia project would thus be one that properly integrates all four. In its field, the term “multimedia” is relatively recent. When multiple mediums are combined, it is used to describe the process. Texts, pictures, animations, videos, and sounds are some of the common features that we may use to identify multimedia. Multimedia is created by combining all of them, but it can also be arranged and presented in other ways. In other terms, multimedia is defined as a combination of several media components into a single topic that benefits the user. Communication is becoming more structured and transparent than ever thanks to all these media components. Today's educational technologists commonly use the word “multimedia” [5]. In the absence of a precise definition, the phrase might also refer to “a provident mix of multiple mass media, such as text, audio, and video,” or it could refer to the creation of computer-based hardware and software products that are mass-produced, yet nonetheless individualize usage and learning.

Multimedia has been described as the coordinated use of a variety of media devices, for as synchronized slides with audiotape. According to Fenrich's definition of multimedia, it is the innovative union of computer hardware and software that enables you to combine video, animation, audio, graphics, and test resources to create powerful presentations on a low-cost desktop computer. Multimedia, in Vaughan's terms, is the combination of text, voice, animation, and videos that are sent by computer or other electronics or digitally altered ways. It is a flawless integration of music, video, graphic art, text, and picture elements that have all been digitally manipulated. Using text and graphics as the presentation materials, multimedia, according to Mayer, is a sort of media used for presentations. Later, he elaborated, saying that multimedia is a kind of media that frequently implicitly mixes and combines a number of components from different media, including music, animation, text, images, and videos [6].

MULTIMEDIA LEARNING ENVIRONMENT

The dynamic aspect of multimedia gives educators the opportunity to improve the traditional “chalk-and-talk” method of instruction by giving students greater freedom to customize their learning approaches. Students can use active involvement, collaboration, and self-exploration to solve problems in a multimedia-based constructivist learning environment. Learning new information is considerably more successfully facilitated by simulations, models, and media-rich study materials with still and animated visuals, videos, and audios combined in an organized manner [7]. It makes it possible for instructors and students to collaborate in a relaxed environment. Both instructors and students now have expanded roles. Additionally, it promotes and boosts individual creativity and innovation as well as peer-learning. Increased interaction between teachers, students, and course materials, as well as creative methods to make learning more dynamic, durable, and applicable to situations outside of the classroom, all contribute to the empowerment of the educational process through multimedia technology. Multimedia evolved during the course of the 1980s and 1990s, becoming a useful tool in instructional technology.

Fig. (2) illustrates the role and impact of multimedia in education. It highlights the significant advancements in hardware and software, including satellite technology, computers, audio, and video, which paved the way for creating new media with immense educational potential.

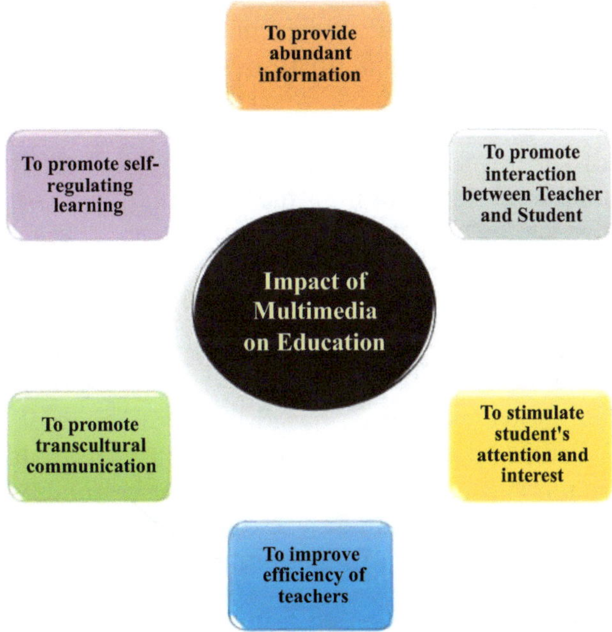

Fig. (2). Impact of multimedia on education.

The figure suggests that these multimedia tools can enhance learning environments by providing improved resources and catering to individual learners' unique needs and preferences. It emphasizes that multimedia can be tailored to accommodate diverse learning styles and create engaging educational experiences.

By leveraging multimedia, educators can incorporate interactive elements, such as videos, animations, simulations, and quizzes, to make learning more interactive and effective. These multimedia tools enable students to visualize complex concepts, engage in hands-on activities, and receive personalized feedback, fostering deeper understanding and knowledge retention.

Overall, Fig. (**2**) emphasizes the significant role and impact of multimedia in education, showcasing how these tools have revolutionized the learning process and opened up new possibilities for personalized and interactive learning experiences.

Using differentiated instruction, multimedia helps students grasp their fundamental abilities. It enables activities in the classroom, learning content management, and administration, and replicates real-world problem-solving contexts. It also allows customized and collaborative learning. Additionally, it facilitates problem-solving by utilizing learning by doing, comprehending abstract ideas, and improving accessibility for remote instructors and learners. The two methods that many colleges and institutes provide to their students with a multimedia education [8]:

1) Integration of several forms of active learning, such as multimodal, two-way data exchange, and other forms of multimedia technology into the classroom;

2) Enhanced content access anytime, anyplace. Media authoring is taught through giving students hands-on experience with multimedia software programmes.

E-LEARNING AND EDUCATIONAL TECHNOLOGY

E-learning, often known as internet-based learning, is a type of institutionalized teaching-based learning that makes use of technological tools such as computers and the internet, intranet (LAN) online education, Computer-based training, and YouTube video-based Learning. The use of computers and the internet is at the core of what is known as "e-learning," although education may take place in a variety of locations, including traditional classrooms [8]. With the assistance of online learning, students have the ability to create and convey new ideas. Outside the classroom, you have always had the opportunity to broaden your knowledge and talents. One of the primary advantages of e-learning is that it contributes to the improvement of advanced skills in both learners and lecturers. For example, eLearning, an educational tool, encourages cooperation by enabling students to collaborate and talk. Instead of sitting in a classroom and listening to professors' lecture for 30 minutes, e-learning students can participate in an online community or platform and study together by communicating with people [9]. Professors are more approachable in this setting and act as mentors to assist students grow as people. This has bridged the gap between instructors and students.

Fig. (**3**) represents the concept of E-Learning, which combines formalized teaching with electronic resources. The figure signifies that E-Learning involves integrating traditional teaching methods and techniques with using electronic tools and resources.

Fig. (3). E-Learning is formed by combining formalized teaching and electronic resources.

By combining formalized teaching, which refers to structured and planned instructional approaches, with electronic resources such as digital platforms, online courses, multimedia materials, and interactive learning tools, E-Learning provides a flexible and accessible learning environment.

The figure suggests integrating formalized teaching and electronic resources in E-Learning, which offers several advantages. It enables learners to access educational content anytime and anywhere, facilitates self-paced learning, promotes interactive and engaging learning experiences, and allows personalized learning paths tailored to individual needs and preferences.

Overall, Fig. (**3**) highlights that E-Learning harnesses the power of technology and instructional design principles to create a blended learning approach that combines traditional teaching methods with electronic resources, ultimately enhancing the accessibility, flexibility, and effectiveness of the learning process.

The study of and moral use of educational technology is the facilitation of learning and enhancement of performance by the development, utilization, and management of suitable technical processes and resources. The most concise and content definition of it is "a collection of instruments that may be useful in student-centered learning" [9]. Instead of being a "Sage on the Stage," it encourages teachers to become "Guides on the Side". The core component of educational technology, sometimes known as "learning technology," is the use of technology throughout the teaching and learning process. Modern learners like to use cutting-edge tools and methods like smart boards, laptop computers, the World Wide Web, smart phones, YouTube, and Wi-Fi. Here, "technology" also refers to efficient and managed to improve e-learning systems, communication and information strategies, teaching methods and management of large groups of students, continuous feedback, and performance evaluations [10].

In Fig. (**4**), the importance and role of e-learning are stated, for example, it is enhancing the level learning and grasping of contents not only in students but also at the same level, teachers are also gaining advantages as they can impart quality content with ease.

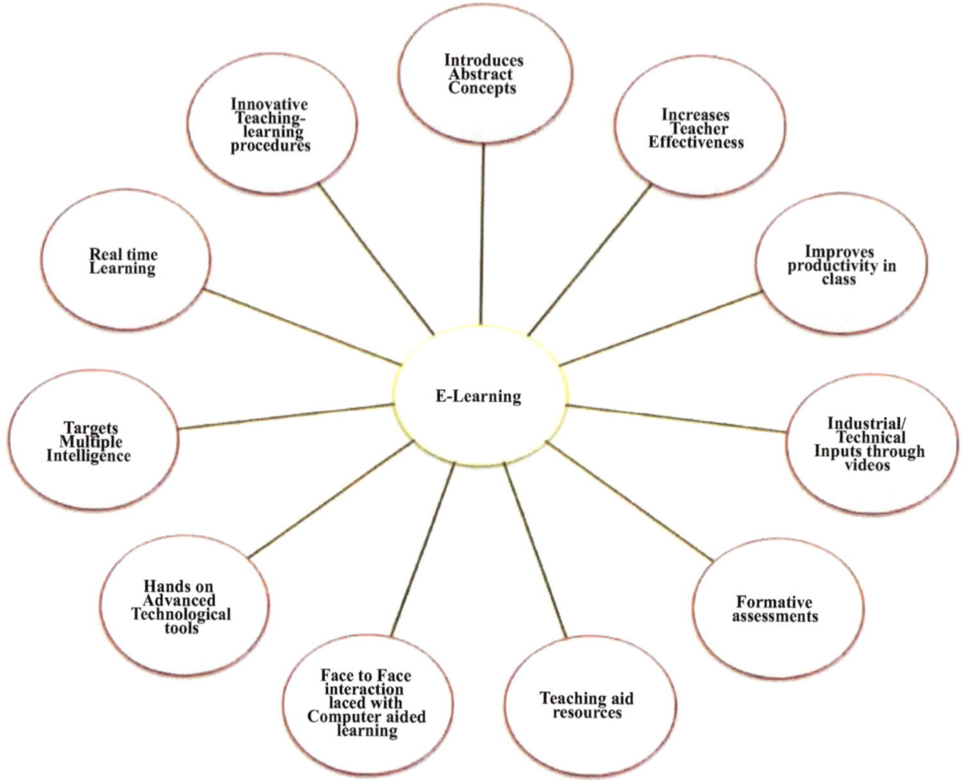

Fig. (4). Advantages of E-Learning.

Multimedia applications may be used in teaching in imaginative and thoughtful ways. The use of multimedia applications is appropriate for many academic disciplines, including cross-curricular ones. The main goal of employing multimedia tools in the classroom is to impart challenging material to people. Students may be taught how to choose and use particular tactics to succeed in any topic by utilizing the "learning to learn" principle. By using this strategy, we hope to boost students' understanding of certain subjects and provide them a reason to learn them. Multimedia learning paradigm involves honing students' abilities and empowering them to face difficulties, develop their personalities, and expand their knowledge. Different interpretations of the "learning to learn" idea can be found depending on basic epistemological and ontological premises [11]. With multimedia, learning may be made more goal-oriented, participative, and flexible in time and place, unaffected by distance, and suited to individual learning styles, as well as increasing teacher-student cooperation. Because multimedia allows teachers to present information in a variety of media, it may be an effective instructional medium for imparting educational content. Multimedia allows for more effective information exchange [12].

INNOVATIVE TEACHING AND LEARNING METHODS

Because technology was created by humans, it is also innovative when an educator utilises it to improve learning. Teachers can use ICT to present multimedia, such as animations, live stream, and other forms, to fit different learning styles. Additionally, ICT enables academic staff to create online courses that allow students to learn at their own speed and in their own environment. To begin with, ICT improves instructors' online or offline teaching approaches. Students are not required to attend a certain class at a specific time; they could learn anytime they like. Second, teaching technology influences students' attitudes toward learning. We become better able to absorb new information, retain it, and use it in practical situations. In conclusion, technology enhances learning by allowing institutions to better respond to students' needs and desires. Excellent teachers teach their pupils both the theory and practice of their subjects. However, the best educators are those who know how to tailor their courses to their pupils' passions. These developments are likely not novel, but they are essential for creative teachers.

Role of ICT

The application of ICT in contemporary life has significantly increased, developed into a crucial tool, and affected the entire learning process. Teachers become more collaborative, competitive, and futuristic by implementing ICT and extending learning outside of the classroom. Through the use of educational ICT, educators have been able to establish learning communities in which educators and subject matter experts from other institutions and countries, students, parents, members of the local community, other educators from the same institution, museums, libraries, and alimony programmes actively participate. The globe has become a village thanks to educational ICT, and digital and remote learning have made it possible for education to easily and at cost effectively permeate communities. Teachers can integrate, coordinate and collaborate with rural and urban learners with professionals and peers, and use educational ICT such as video conferencing, online chats and group social media sites to ensure that classroom learning is relevant. ICT provided a platform for academic participants and motivated students to participate meaningfully. It offers students access to high-quality educational tools and materials regardless of their location. By using a mixed learning strategy, it is improving learners' learning experiences. ICT is also making it easier for students to connect with non-academic resources and manage the issues in their personal lives that could interfere with their ability to learn. Additionally, it promotes the active involvement of disabled students in educational programmes and other learning resources, notably in higher education.

Blockchain Technology Impact

Data storage is just one advantage that the Distributed Ledger Technology (DLT) from blockchain offers to education. The amount of storage is theoretically infinite since each time new data is added, it creates another "block" to the system. The data will be dispersed throughout the system's many computers while also being encrypted. Data exchange becomes decentralized and transparent as a result. Massive Open Online Courses (MOOCs) and ePortfolios leverage blockchain technology to validate students' skills and knowledge. For eLearning agencies, the DLT systems will provide solutions to the issues of authentication, scale, and affordability. Additionally, it can assist student applicants in publishing their successes when they are looking for work.

Importance of Big Data

The cognitive development must be individualized in order to meet the demands of the learners. Additionally, with the success of online education and COVID-19, we now have more data than ever. To create and offer the course in an appropriate format, instructional designers have access to pertinent information about learners' experiences. The course's content, learners enrolment, learners' performance (course time, completion, exam result), and learners' feedback are some details to look for.

Fig. (**5**) shows a reflection of AI and how it changes the education system.

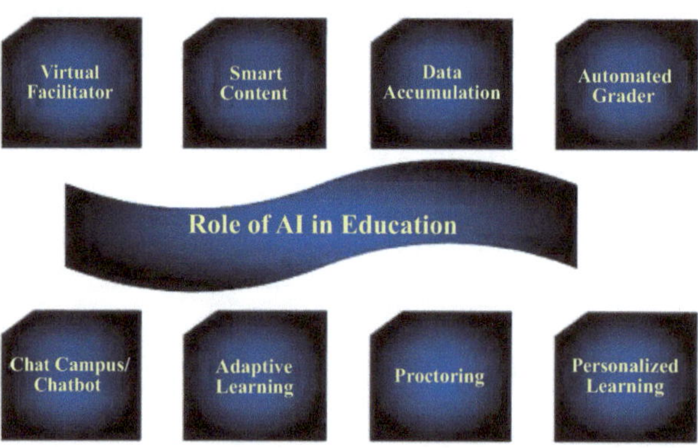

Fig. (5). How AI is changing the face of education.

Advent of Artificial Intelligence(AI)

In the US EdTech sector right now, AI is the "it" thing. According to predictions, AI will likely dominate trends through 2021 and expand by more than 45%. So why one of the biggest EdTech marketplaces in the world are experiencing a trend boom? The primary use of AI in education is to automate routine tasks like grading. Assessments of multiple-choice and fill-in-the-blank questions can now be automated by teachers. As a result, computerized writing assessments of kids may not be far behind.

AI is also beneficial for educators and students. For example, if a teacher is too busy to take care of everyone, a student can get support from her AI tutor. AI-driven systems can provide useful feedback to both students and teachers. For this reason, some schools are using AI systems to track student progress and alert teachers to potential performance problems. Therefore, AI is unlikely to be a useful tool for teaching.

Informatics for Learning

Particularly for higher education, the contemporary environment of learning analytics has radically changed. Through the use of learning analytics, educators can monitor and report on students' progress online. They can use such information to maximize their understanding of learning. Teachers can enhance their students' knowledge and skill acquisition by reading insights from the learning processes of their people. For instance, teachers can determine what information—text, pictures, infographics, or videos—students prefer and utilize more in subsequent courses. Additionally, teachers can identify the knowledge components that were not effectively conveyed and improve them the following time. Additionally, learning analytics aids educators in locating groups of kids who might be experiencing behavioral or academic difficulties.

STEAM

STEAM-based education is the newest IT development that goes beyond STEM-based curricular topics. This new direction in ICT uses Science, Engineering, Design, Art (the new element), and Math (the old element) to tackle real-world issues *via* hands-on learning and creative problem-solving. As a primary advantage, STEAM education fosters children's natural curiosity in the world around them. In addition, it creates a safe space for students to test out their theories and expand their horizons. When individuals are confident in their own individual approaches to learning, they are better equipped to work together effectively.

Use of Social Media

Social networking sites are now widely used in educational institutions as a communication tool so that students may readily communicate with one another. Shared study materials, group discussions, and simple commenting are all options available to students. Even an animated educational video has the potential to go viral online. TedEd is a prime illustration of this pattern. The educational videos produced by this group are posted on YouTube where individuals may quickly access, find, and share them with their peers. Social media is here to stay and foster a culture of sharing and cooperation, which enhances the educational process.

RECENT ADVANCEMENTS AND BENEFITS OF MULTIMEDIA LEARNING

According to several studies that looked into how ICT is affecting education, multimedia technology has a favorable influence on how professors teach and how students understand subject matter. Multimedia apps are used in education as a data source to provide learning tools to students. Applications that utilize multimedia are also used to boost learning and facilitate interaction between students and faculty. Various benefits of multimedia learning are listed below in Fig. (**6**).

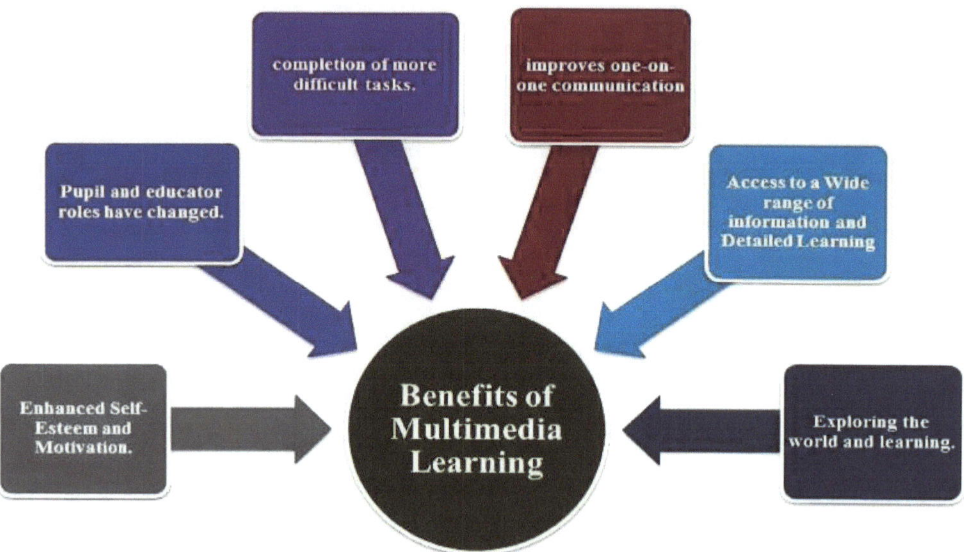

Fig. (6). Benefits of multimedia learning.

The value of the worldwide education technology market is projected to reach USD 106.46 billion in 2021 and is anticipated to increase at a compound annual growth rate (CAGR) of 16.4% since 2022 through 2030. The term "educational technology" (EdTech) can refer to either the hardware or the software that is utilized to instruct learners digitally. It helps learners overcome difficulties through the use of technology in learning and teaching E-books and other forms of educational content that can be opened online anywhere in the world. Online study material is easier to create than paper study material that is expensive to produce. A large user base can easily translate and access readily available digital books in a variety of languages. In addition, students can listen to audio versions of the material to increase their vocabulary and develop better interpretive reading skills, especially for students with physical disabilities. For example, OrbitNote, a PDF-enabled app, was released in January 2022 by Texthelp Ltd., a well-known provider of assistive technology for the EdTech sector.

Fig. (7) shows the "Education Technology Market Size, Share, and Trends Analysis Report." My responses are based on general knowledge and understanding until September 2021.

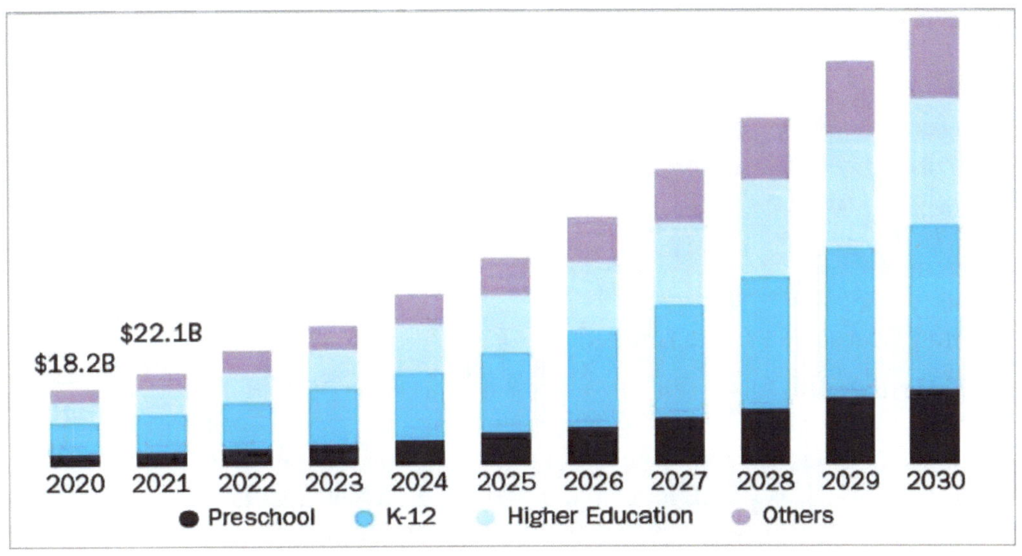

Fig. (7). Education Technology Market Size, Share, and Trends Analysis Report, By End-User(Business, Consumer), Forecasts for segments by kind, deployment, region, and year, 2022 to 2030.

It would be great if visually impaired students could record voice notes and access documents. It is anticipated that EdTech products will advance with emerging technologies such as the Internet of Things (IoT), artificial intelligence (AI), and augmented reality (AR/VR), and will substantially contribute to the growth of the industry. By incorporating AR and VR into her EdTech solutions, she can provide immersive experiences for her learners. For example, in January 2022, a new AR/VR learning device was launched by zSpace, Inc., a US-based EdTech company that offers hybrid or distance learning. MyClassCampus, an ERP platform for educational companies, was purchased by Teachmint Technologies Pvt. Ltd in January 2022 as per the reports. Teachmint Technologies Pvt Ltd is the company behind an online programme that is designed for use by both students and educators. As a direct result of this purchase, Teachmint will be able to increase the variety of services it provides to schools and other types of educational institutions by integrating its enterprise resource planning (ERP) software with its learning management system (LMS). Additionally, BYJU'S, an EdTech company that offers online tuition, teamed with Google LLC in June 2021 to improve the consistency of online learning for both teachers and students. Through this agreement, educational institutions will be able to provide students with a customized digital platform for class management. Leading companies in the global market for education technology include:

- BYJU’s
- Blackboard Inc.
- Chegg, Inc.
- Coursera Inc.
- EduTech
- edX Inc.
- Google LLC
- Instructure, Inc.
- Microsoft
- Udacity, Inc.
- upGrad Education Private Limited

CONCLUSION

In the field of education, two essential components include multimedia and learning theory. It is possible to make good use of multimedia as a learning tool due to the fact that it typically serves to encourage users and improve interaction between multimedia apps and their respective users. As a matter of fact, one of the ultimate purposes of using multimedia in language instruction is to increase the student's desire and interest in studying, which is a practical approach to include them in the subject matter learning process. It is anticipated that the application of multimedia in educational settings will continue to grow in the next years from the point of view of the progression of technology. Aside from some issues, effective use of multimedia technology in the classroom is possible only if teachers have computer skills if the financial problems of building the infrastructure are overcome, and if teachers do not become anti-technology. I can do it. Technology is advancing rapidly and is beginning to offer educators a wealth of potential tools. The future of education depends on finding technology that gives students a positive learning experience.

REFERENCES

[1] O.M.K. Alhawi, J. Baldwin, and A. Dehghantanha, Leveraging machine learning techniques for windows ransomware networktraffic detection. *Cyber Threat Intelligence.* Springer: Cham, Switzerland, 2018, pp. 93-106. [http://dx.doi.org/10.1007/978-3-319-73951-9_5]

[2] B.M. Khammas, "Ransomware detection using random forest technique", *ICT Express,* vol. 6, no. 4, pp. 325-331, 2020. [http://dx.doi.org/10.1016/j.icte.2020.11.001]

[3] J.A. Herrera-Silva, and M. Hernández-Álvarez, "Dynamic feature dataset for ransomware detection using machine learning algorithms", *Sensors,* vol. 23, no. 3, p. 1053, 2023. [http://dx.doi.org/10.3390/s23031053] [PMID: 36772092]

[4] J. Hwang, J. Kim, S. Lee, and K. Kim, "Two-Stage ransomware detection using dynamic analysis and machine learning techniques", *Wirel. Pers. Commun.,* vol. 112, no. 4, pp. 2597-2609, 2020. [http://dx.doi.org/10.1007/s11277-020-07166-9]

[5] S.K. Shaukat, and V.J. Ribeiro, "RansomWall: A layered defense system against cryptographic ransomware attacks using machinelearning", *2018 10th International Conference on Communication Systems & Networks,* 2018, Bengaluru, India, pp. 356-363. [http://dx.doi.org/10.1109/COMSNETS.2018.8328219]

[6] M. Hirano, R. Hodota, and R. Kobayashi, "RanSAP: An open dataset of ransomware storage access patterns for training machine learning models", *Forensic Science International: Digital Investigation,* vol. 40, p. 301314, 2022. [http://dx.doi.org/10.1016/j.fsidi.2021.301314]

[7] S.I. Bae, G.B. Lee, and E.G. Im, "Ransomware detection using machine learning algorithms", *Concurr. Comput.,* vol. 32, no. 18, pp. 1-11, 2020. [http://dx.doi.org/10.1002/cpe.5422]

[8] Y. Takeuchi, K. Sakai, and S. Fukumoto, "Detecting ransomware using support vector machines", *In Proceedings of the 47th International Conference on Parallel Processing Companion* August 2018, pp.1-6 . [http://dx.doi.org/10.1145/3229710.3229726]

[9] F.A. Narudin, A. Feizollah, N.B. Anuar, and A. Gani, "Evaluation of machine learning classifiers for mobile malware detection", *Soft Comput.,* vol. 20, no. 1, pp. 343-357, 2016. [http://dx.doi.org/10.1007/s00500-014-1511-6]

[10] Available From: https://www.windows-commandline.com/enable-disable-system-resoreservice/#:~:text=Disable%20System%20restore%20service%20from%20command%20line%20We,command%20line%20you%20can%20run%20the%20below%20command

[11] Available From: https://www.cyberithub.com/20-useful-wmic-command-exampls-in-windows-cheat-sheet/

[12] Available From: https://sensorstechforum.com/ransomware-virus-what-is-it/

CHAPTER 8

Emerging AI Trends in Intelligent and Interactive Multimedia Systems

P. Devisivasankari[1,*] and **R. Vijayakumar**[1]

[1] *CMR Institute of Technology, Bengaluru, India*

Abstract: Intelligent and interactive multimedia systems are in a constant state of evolution, with new technologies and developments being introduced daily. AI is a fundamental enabler of these technologies, providing intelligence and interactivity required to make them more useful and user-friendly. This article examines the current state of AI-based intelligent and interactive multimedia systems, highlighting the most promising trends and obstacles. Then, we explore emerging AI trends that are anticipated to play a significant role in overcoming these obstacles and enabling the development of new and more complex intelligent and interactive multimedia systems.

Keywords: Educational, ICT, Information and technology, Multimedia, Simulations, Technology, Teacher training.

INTRODUCTION

With the use of artificial intelligence (AI) algorithms, we can generate new content, such as photographs, videos, and text. Explainable AI refers to the usage of AI systems that can explain their decision-making process, which aids in establishing user confidence. The use of Multi-modal systems is intended to make the integration of several modalities, such as vision, speech, and language, to provide interactions that are more realistic and human-like [1]. The following are emerging AI trends for intelligent and interactive multimedia systems:

Deep Learning entails the application of deep neural networks to image and video processing, natural language processing, and speech recognition.

Computer Vision: The application of artificial intelligence systems to analyse, comprehend, and interpret visual data from the real world, such as photographs and videos.

* **Corresponding author P. Devisivasankari:** CMR Institute of Technology, Bengaluru, India; E-mail: devisivasankari.p@cmrit.ac.in

Suman Kumar Swarnkar, Sapna Singh Kshatri, Virendra Kumar Swarnkar & Tien Anh Tran (Eds.)

Natural Language Processing (NLP) is the use of artificial intelligence (AI) systems to analyse, comprehend, and synthesize human language, such as speech and text.

Reinforcement Learning: The application of artificial intelligence (AI) algorithms that learn *via* trial and error, enabling systems to adapt and improve over time.

Fig. (**1**) explains Multimedia Intelligence, which focuses on the advancements and developments in AI that aim to overcome obstacles in intelligent and interactive multimedia systems.

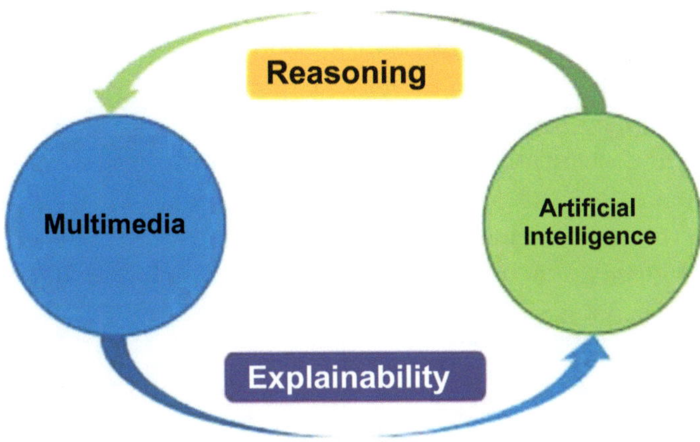

Fig. (1). Multimedia Intelligence [1].

There are a number of AI developments aimed at overcoming the obstacles in intelligent and interactive multimedia systems, including: Natural Language Processing (NLP) that is used to enhance the interaction between users and multimedia systems by permitting them to communicate in natural language. Computer vision is used to allow multimedia systems to comprehend and interpret visual data, such as photos and videos. Deep Learning is used to enhance the ability of multimedia systems to learn and adapt to new data. Reinforcement learning is used to enhance the decision-making abilities of multimedia systems by permitting them to learn from their experiences. Generative models such as GANs and VAEs are used to enhance the capacity of multimedia systems to generate and create new content. Explainable AI is used to increase the interpretability and transparency of multimedia systems, making it easier for people to comprehend how and why the system makes certain judgments. Fig. (**1**) depicts the MM intelligence in interactive systems.

ROLE OF DL, ML IN INTELLIGENT AND INTERACTIVE MULTIMEDIA SYSTEMS

These developments aim to make multimedia systems smarter and more interactive by enhancing their capacity to comprehend, process, and generate multimedia content. Developing intelligent and interactive multimedia systems has numerous obstacles, including Natural language comprehension, which is the capability of a computer system to comprehend and interpret human language in a manner similar to that of a person. Multimodal integration is the incorporation of diverse modalities, such as text, audio, and video, and the interpretation of the information they supply. Personalization is the process of tailoring user experiences depending on their choices and behaviour. Interactivity is the design of interfaces that are user-friendly and intuitive. Adaptability: the capacity of a system to adapt to changing user circumstances and requirements. Scalability is the capacity to manage big volumes of data and a large number of concurrent users. Privacy and security: safeguarding user information and protecting the system from harmful attacks. Fig. (**2**) depicts that AI is a major enabling technology for interactive multimedia systems because it enables the development of intelligent and responsive systems that can adapt to the users' demands and preferences.

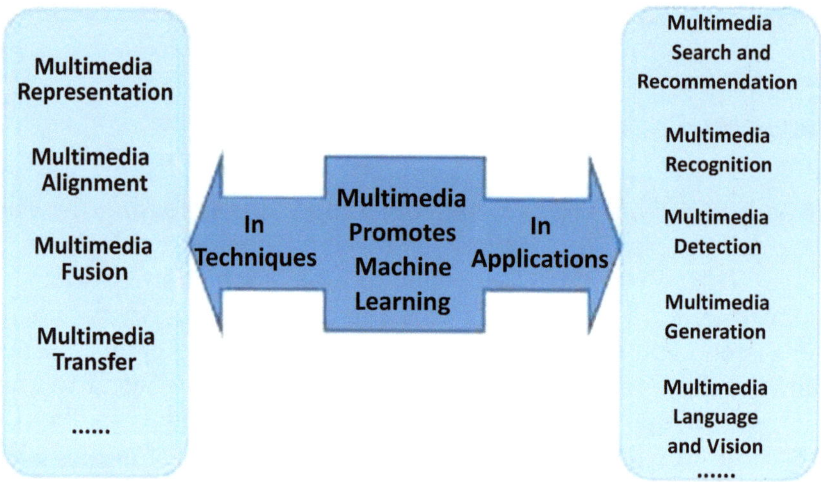

Fig. (2). How multimedia promotes machine learning [2].

SPECIFIC APPLICATIONS OF AI

Natural Language Processing uses NLP approaches powered by artificial intelligence. Multimedia systems can comprehend and respond to user input in natural language. This enables more natural and intuitive system interfaces, such as voice commands and text-based queries. Computer vision techniques driven by artificial intelligence can be utilised to enable multimedia systems to evaluate and comprehend visual input, such as photographs and videos. This enables more precise and responsive visual identification, including face detection, object recognition, and scene comprehension. Using machine learning approaches powered by artificial intelligence, multimedia systems can learn from data such as user interactions and preferences [3 - 7]. This enables the development of more tailored and adaptable systems, such as recommender systems, individualised content distribution, and adaptive user interfaces. Using AI-powered techniques, multimedia systems can comprehend and respond to human behaviour and emotions. This enables more natural and intuitive interactions with the system, including gesture recognition, emotion detection, and customised feedback. Fig. (**3**) depicts how AI plays a significant role in enhancing the intelligence and responsiveness of interactive multimedia systems like audio-visual process, allowing for more natural and intuitive interactions between humans and technology. The current state of the art in AI-based intelligent and interactive multimedia systems is progressing rapidly, with new technologies and advancements in a range of fields.

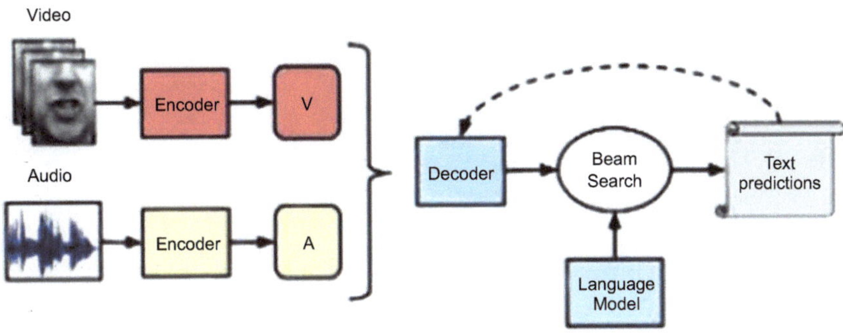

Fig. (3). Multimedia use in AVR process.

Existing systems that exhibit the present state of the art include the following:

Intelligent Virtual Assistants: Apple's Siri, Amazon's Alexa, and Google's Assistant use natural language processing (NLP) to comprehend and respond to user voice requests. These systems are capable of a variety of functions, including organising appointments, playing music, and controlling smart gadgets. Intelligent Video Analytics: Computer vision is employed by AI-powered video analytics systems, such as those used in surveillance and security, to evaluate and interpret camera visual input. These systems are capable of object detection, facial recognition, and anomaly detection, among other things. Intelligent Recommender Systems: Netflix and YouTube utilise AI-powered recommender systems to recommend material to viewers based on their viewing history and preferences. These systems can also customise the user experience [8 - 10] by delivering customised content suggestions and customizable user interfaces. Intelligent Chatbots: AI-powered chatbots, such as those employed by customer service departments, use natural language processing (NLP) (Fig. **4**) and machine learning (ML) to understand and respond to user input in a human-like manner, automating customer service interactions and enhancing the customer experience.

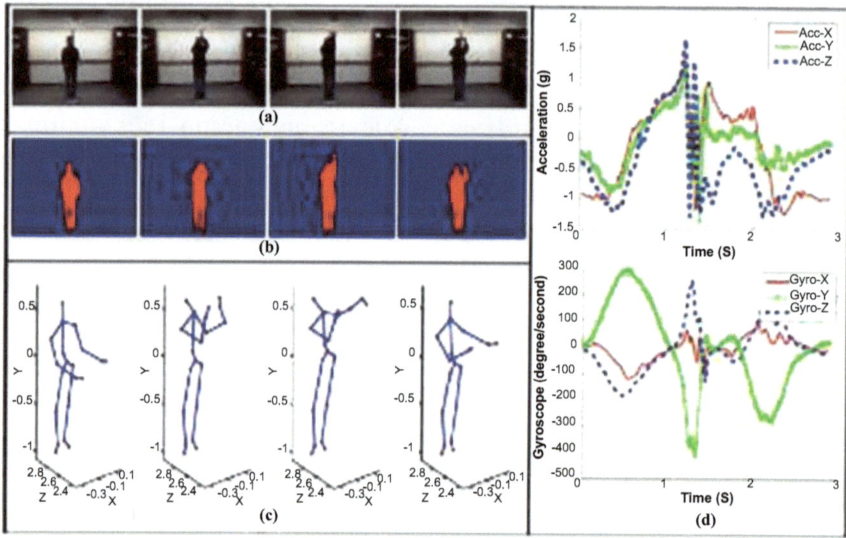

Fig. (4). action based Multimodality input for basketball shoot.

Intelligent Multimodal Interaction systems: AI-powered multimodal systems, such as Google Duplex, use AI approaches to comprehend and generate several modalities, such as speech, text, and images, in order to give users with more intuitive and natural interactions.

ENHANCE THE NATURALNESS, SCALABILITY, AND CUSTOMIZATION OF INTELLIGENT AND INTERACTIVE MULTIMEDIA SYSTEMS

These are but a few instances of the present state of the art in AI-based intelligent and interactive multimedia systems, and new developments are being made in this field on a daily basis. Certainly, here are some instances of existing intelligent and interactive multimedia systems based on AI: Amazon Echo and Google Home are examples of voice-controlled smart speakers that utilise AI-powered natural language processing (NLP) to comprehend and respond to user voice instructions. These gadgets are capable of a variety of functions, including playing music, controlling smart home devices, and presenting information. Intelligent Video Surveillance: Many video surveillance systems now analyse and interpret visual input from cameras using AI-powered computer vision. These systems are capable of object detection, facial recognition, and anomaly detection, among other things. Intelligent Personalized News Feed: Social media sites such as Facebook and Twitter employ machine learning algorithms powered by artificial intelligence to personalise the news feed for each user. Based on a user's surfing history and engagement patterns, they can display pertinent news, videos, and posts. Intelligent Virtual Personal Shopping Assistants: Numerous online merchants now use intelligent virtual personal shopping assistants that may aid clients in locating products, recommending related things, and answering inquiries about product features, availability, and specifications. Intelligent Interactive Multimodal Systems: AI-powered multimodal systems, such as Google Duplex, use AI approaches to interpret and generate several modalities, such as speech, text, and images, in order to give users more intuitive and natural interactions. Numerous video games currently employ AI-powered approaches to produce more realistic and entertaining gaming worlds. For instance, games such as Grand Theft Auto V and Red Dead Redemption 2 use AI to generate NPCs with different personalities and behaviours that are more genuine and realistic.

Intelligent and interactive multimedia systems:

These are just a few examples of the numerous intelligent and interactive multimedia systems currently available that are based on artificial intelligence. Fig. (**5**) is for human computer interaction. As the science of AI continues to progress, it is possible that more complex and sophisticated systems will be created in the future. Researchers and developers are now attempting to address a number of significant obstacles and restrictions of AI-based intelligent and interactive multimedia systems.

Naturalness: Making the interactions between people and systems more natural and intuitive is one of the primary problems of AI-based intelligent multimedia systems. This includes enhancing the ability of systems to comprehend and respond to natural language, as well as creating more human-like user interfaces. Scalability: Another problem is to make AI-based intelligent multimedia systems more scalable, so that they can accommodate massive volumes of data and users. This entails building new architectures and infrastructures to handle large-scale systems as well as enhancing the efficiency existing algorithms [11 - 14].

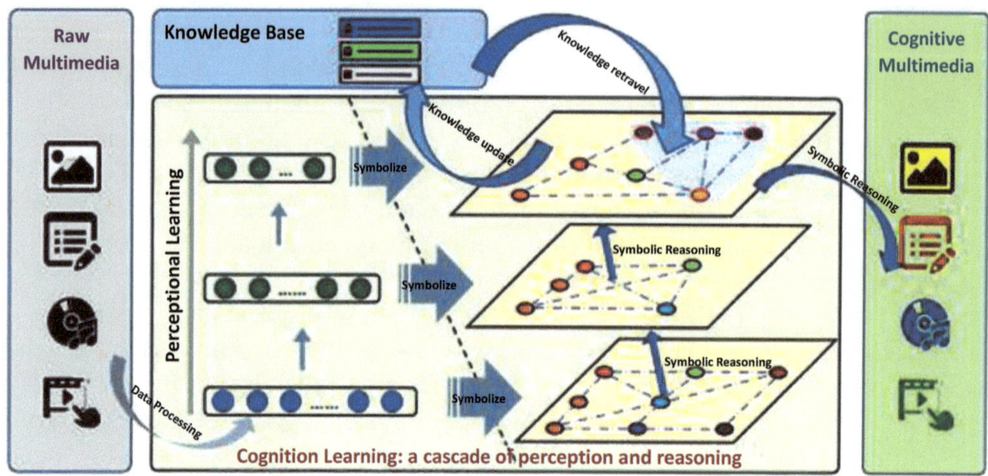

Fig. (5). AI using HCI.

Explainability and interpretability: AI-based systems can be opaque and complicated, making it difficult for users and engineers to comprehend how they function. This is a serious difficulty, especially when it comes to establishing trust in AI-based systems in high-stakes fields such as healthcare and finance. Personalization: Another obstacle is to personalize AI-based intelligent multimedia systems for the user. This includes the development of algorithms that can learn from the user's interactions and preferences, as well as the creation of interfaces that can adapt to the user's needs and preferences. As AI-based intelligent multimedia systems collect, process, and store vast quantities of personal data, guaranteeing the privacy and security of this data is essential. This includes preventing unwanted access to the data and ensuring that it is utilized ethically and in accordance with applicable legislation. The application of multimodal input [1] was used for context model by xin wang [1]. Intelligent multimedia systems based on AI frequently require considerable user testing and iteration to guarantee that the final product is usable, effective, and user-friendly. This can be a considerable obstacle, especially given the field's rapid evolution and the complexity of the technology for non-specialists. These obstacles are not insurmountable, and researchers and developers are continually pursuing innovative solutions. To construct truly intelligent and interactive systems that are natural, scalable, and personalised, the considerable effort remains. There are numerous approaches to overcoming the obstacles and constraints of AI-based intelligent and interactive multimedia systems, including: Deep learning is a sort of machine learning that employs neural networks to acquire knowledge from data. It has demonstrated considerable potential for enhancing the naturalness of

AI-based intelligent multimedia systems by enabling them to comprehend and respond to natural words, images, and videos.

Fig. (**6**) is generated based on general knowledge and understanding.

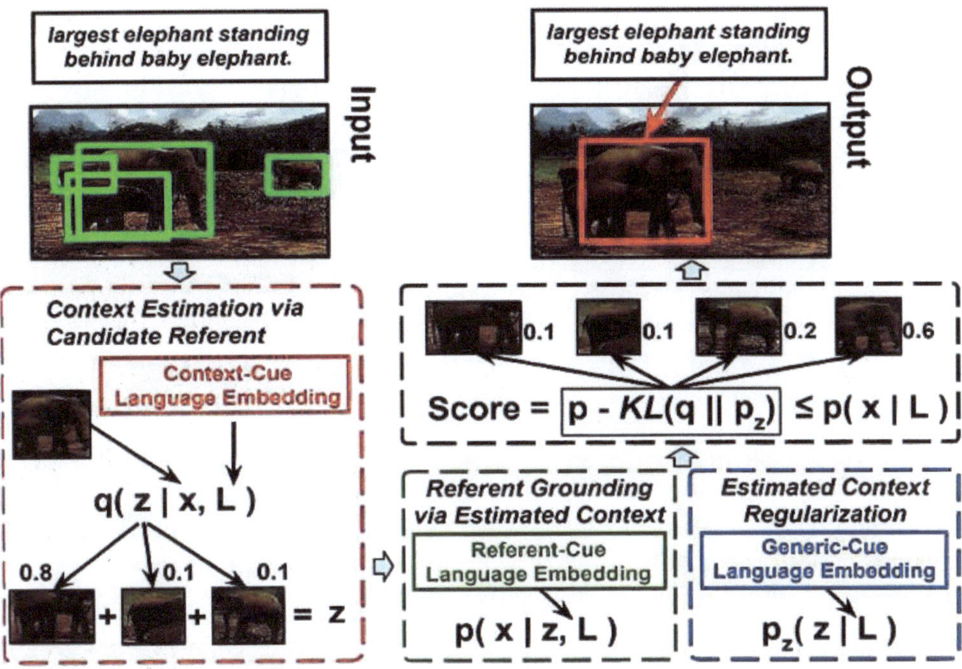

Fig. (6). context model for multimodal alignment [1].

Reinforcement Learning: Reinforcement learning is a sort of machine learning that entails teaching systems to act in an environment so as to maximise a reward. It can be used to enhance the scalability of AI-based intelligent multimedia systems by enabling them to learn from user interactions and adapt to various settings [14 - 17]. Transfer learning is a technique that permits a model learned on one job to be utilised as a starting point for a model trained on a separate but related activity. This can be used to improve the personalization of AI-based intelligent multimedia systems by permitting them to learn from a variety of users and tasks. Explainable AI: Explainable AI (XAI) strategies strive to make AI models more interpretable so that the user can comprehend the system's decision-making process. This can be utilised to enhance the explainability and interpretability of AI-based intelligent multimedia systems, as well as to raise user confidence in the system. Human-centered design is an approach to the development of technology that focuses on the user's needs, desires, and limits.

This method can help overcome the constraints of AI-based intelligent multimedia systems by ensuring that the final product is usable, effective, and user-friendly. Privacy and protection: It is essential to establish comprehensive security measures and data encryption, in addition to complying with applicable rules, in order to protect the privacy and security of personal data. In order to develop users' confidence, it is essential to be upfront about data collecting, usage, and storage practises. These are a few examples of how academics and developers are attempting to overcome the difficulties and constraints of AI-based intelligent and interactive multimedia systems. Notably, these solutions are not mutually exclusive, and many AI-based intelligent multimedia systems will likely employ a combination of these techniques to accomplish the desired results.

Deep learning is a sort of machine learning that uses neural networks to learn from data, and it has demonstrated enormous potential for enhancing the naturalness of AI-based intelligent and interactive multimedia systems. Listed below are a few specific applications of deep learning to intelligent and interactive multimedia systems [18 - 22].

NLP: Natural Language Processing Deep learning can enhance the capacity of intelligent and interactive multimedia systems to comprehend and respond to natural language. This covers speech recognition, natural language comprehension, and machine translation. Deep learning can be used to enhance the capacity of intelligent and interactive multimedia systems to evaluate and comprehend visual input such as photographs and videos. This includes item identification, face recognition, and scene comprehension. Deep learning can improve the ability of intelligent and interactive multimedia systems to evaluate and comprehend auditory input, such as voice and music. This includes tasks such as speech recognition, speaker identification, and classification of musical genres. Deep learning can be used to enhance the capacity of intelligent and interactive multimedia systems to comprehend and respond to human behaviour and emotions. This includes gesture recognition, emotion detection, and individualised feedback. Interactivity of Multimodal Systems: Deep learning can be used to enhance the capacity of intelligent and interactive multimodal systems to comprehend and generate numerous modalities, such as speech, text, and images, in order to deliver more intuitive and natural user interactions. Deep learning enables computers to learn from vast volumes of data, resulting in enhanced performance and more precise outcomes. In addition, deep learning models may automatically learn features from the data, which eliminates the need for feature engineering, a time-consuming and domain-specific activity. Deep learning has shown considerable promise in enhancing the naturalness of AI-based intelligent and interactive multimedia systems, however, it is neither a panacea nor the only option. Many intelligent and interactive multimedia systems will likely use a combination of deep learning and other AI techniques to accomplish the desired outcomes.

Reinforcement learning is a sort of machine learning involving the training of systems to act in a given environment so as to maximise a reward [23 - 25]. It can be used to enhance the scalability of AI-based intelligent and interactive multimedia systems by enabling them to learn from user interactions and adapt to various settings. Listed below are a few specific applications of reinforcement learning to intelligent and interactive multimedia systems. Intelligent and interactive multimedia systems can be trained using reinforcement learning to adapt their user interfaces to the needs and preferences of individual users. A system could, for instance, learn to offer information or alternatives in a manner that is most likely to be successful for a given user, based on their previous interactions.

Personalized Content Recommendation: Intelligent and interactive multimedia systems can be trained through reinforcement learning to propose content to users based on their preferences and interactions. The algorithm can adapt its recommendations in response to user feedback, such as likes and clicks. Reinforcement learning can be used to teach intelligent and interactive multimedia systems how to play games like chess and Go. The system is capable of learning from its own experience and modifying its techniques to become more effective over time.

Robotics: Intelligent and interactive multimedia systems can be trained using reinforcement learning to control robots such as drones or autonomous vehicles. The system can learn to make judgments and operate in a manner that optimises a reward, such as keeping inside a specified region or avoiding obstacles. Adaptive Streaming: Reinforcement learning can be used to optimise the quality of service in multimedia streaming systems by adjusting the streaming rate, resolution, and other parameters according to network conditions and user preferences.

Reinforcement learning has shown considerable promise in enhancing the scalability of AI-based intelligent and interactive multimedia systems, but it is neither a panacea nor the only option. In fact, many intelligent and interactive multimedia systems will likely combine reinforcement learning with other AI techniques to produce the desired outcomes. In addition, reinforcement learning can be computationally costly and requires a large amount of data to train the model, which can be a constraint in certain circumstances. The topic of interactive multimedia is always expanding, and there are numerous unanswered research questions and potential future paths. Here are a few instances:

Human-centered AI: Creating AI-based intelligent and interactive multimedia systems that are more natural and intuitive for users to interact with and can adapt to the user's requirements, preferences, and emotions is a significant research challenge. The development of AI-based intelligent and interactive multimedia systems that are transparent and interpretable, allowing the user to comprehend the reasoning behind the system's decisions, is an important area of research. Scalability: Developing AI-based intelligent and interactive multimedia systems that can manage vast volumes of data and users, as well as scale too many devices and platforms, is a significant research problem. Developing AI-based intelligent and interactive multimedia systems that can comprehend and generate numerous modalities, such as speech, text, and images, is a research problem since it needs the integration of different AI methodologies.

Personalization: It is a research problem to develop AI-based intelligent and interactive multimedia systems that can personalise the user experience through the provision of customised content recommendations and individualised user interfaces.

Privacy and security: Ensuring the privacy and security of personal data in AI-based intelligent and interactive multimedia systems is a key research topic, as it requires the implementation of effective security protocols, data encryption, and compliance with applicable rules.

Human-computer interaction: It is a research problem to develop AI-based intelligent and interactive multimedia systems that can comprehend and respond to human behaviour and emotions, and can provide more natural and intuitive interactions. The development of AI-based intelligent and interactive multimedia systems that can employ AR and VR technologies to provide more immersive and interactive user experiences is a problem in the field of study.

Multimodal interaction: Developing multimedia interactive systems that can comprehend and generate multiple modalities, such as speech, text, images, and gestures, is a research challenge because it requires the integration of different modalities and the ability to comprehend the interaction's context.

FUTURE SCOPES

The traditional Turing Test has a variant known as the Test of the Turing Machine for Multimedia, which evaluates a machine's capacity to comprehend and respond to multimedia inputs such as images, videos, and audio. The Multimedia Turing Test is another name for the Test of the Turing Machine for Multimedia. The purpose of the evaluation is to assess whether or not the machine is capable of responding to the same kinds of multimedia inputs in a manner that is indistinguishable from a human's reaction. There are currently no standardised versions of the test because it is still in the process of being developed. The Multimedia Turing Test is just one method that can be used to determine how intelligent a multimedia system is; however, it is not the only method. Activities that require the machine to evaluate, understand, and generate multimedia content, as well as tasks that need the machine to make judgments based on multimedia inputs, are some other ways that can be used to measure multimedia intelligence. This inquiry has the ability to investigate the prospective uses of multimedia intelligence in domains such as entertainment, education, and communications, in addition to analysing and quantifying the level of multimedia intelligence that is present. In addition to this, it might explore the ethical and sociological consequences of machines that can interpret and generate multimedia content, as well as the obstacles and limits associated with constructing such machines.

VISUAL TURING TEST

The standard Turing test has a variant known as the visual Turing test, which analyses a machine's capacity to comprehend and respond to visual inputs like pictures and movies. This test is a variation of the original Turing test. The purpose of the evaluation is to assess whether or not the replies of the computer to the visual cues can be distinguished from the responses of a human. A human evaluator would first offer the machine with visual stimuli as part of a visual Turing test, and then they would ask the machine questions or have it execute tasks based on the visual stimuli that they had shown it. The evaluator would next compare the replies of the machine to those of a human in order to assess whether or not it is possible to discriminate between the two. You may give the computer a picture and then ask it to explain what it sees as an example of a visual Turing test. The description provided by the machine would then be contrasted with the description provided by a person of the identical image. If there is no discernible difference between the two descriptions, then the machine has passed the visual Turing test. The Visual Turing test has potential applications in a wide variety of domains, including computer vision, object recognition, autonomous vehicles, picture and video analysis, and many more.

Recent Developments made in the Turing Test for Multimedia

Recent developments in the Turing test for multimedia have focused on developing more sophisticated methods for evaluating a machine's ability to understand and respond to multimedia inputs. These developments have been made possible by recent advancements in computer processing power. The use of deep learning and neural networks to train machines on massive datasets of multimedia content, such as photographs and videos, in order to improve the machines' capacity to comprehend and generate multimedia content is one technique that has been adopted .The development of more advanced evaluation methods, such as employing several human evaluators or including subjective measurements, is another strategy that has been adopted in order to properly evaluate the multimedia intelligence of a machine. In addition, some researchers are investigating the use of virtual reality and augmented reality in the context of multimedia Turing tests. This would make it possible to conduct evaluations of a machine's multimedia intelligence that are more immersive and interesting for the user. In general, both the fields of multimedia intelligence and the multimedia Turing test are thriving research fields, and new discoveries and advancements are consistently made in both of these areas.

An Explanation of Justification in Multimedia Formats

The development of more explainable reasoning methods for multimedia will be an important area of focus for research in the years to come, and it is deserving of more investigation. The incorporation of reasoning characteristics into deep neural networks can be accomplished through the basic method of supplementing deep neural networks with other reasoning features. It would be beneficial for deep neural networks to be equipped with additional reasoning-augmented layers or modules. This would enhance the capacity of deep neural networks to represent data. Heterogeneous networks, for instance, can connect a wide variety of multimedia artefacts, which can then be represented using GNNs.

Automated Forms of Both Machine and Meta-Learning

Both the academic and industrial research communities are conducting exciting research in the disciplines of Automated Machine Learning (AutoML) and Meta-learning, both of which are seeing tremendous expansion. The purpose of AutoML is to automate the process of applying end-to-end machine learning models to problems that are encountered in the real world. The idea behind AutoML is that a computer system ought to be able to automatically adjust itself to new data, tasks, and environments. This is something that people are quite good at, therefore it makes sense that a computer should be able to do the same.

Digital Retinas

A digital retina is a specific kind of artificial neural network that was developed to simulate the way in which the human retina processes visual information. The human retina is the layer of the back of the eye that is responsible for detecting light and converting it into electrical impulses that the brain can then interpret as information regarding vision. A digital retina employs a similar method to evaluate visual information, such as images or videos, in order to extract relevant elements or patterns. Examples of this type of information include photographs and moving videos. Image enhancement, object detection, and other forms of picture processing can all be accomplished with the help of digital retinas, which can also be utilised for image recognition. They can also be used to improve the performance of other types of artificial neural networks, such as convolutional neural networks (CNNs), by pre-processing visual information and providing a more robust set of features for the CNN to analyse. Artificial neurons, silicon retinas, and memristors are just a few of the many technologies that can be utilised to bring about the creation of a digital retina in either hardware or software. They find widespread application in computer vision, robotics, and automation research and development. There are a great number of distinct varieties of digital retinas, each of which possesses an architecture and characteristics that are entirely unique to themselves. Others are designed to be highly accurate and are capable of achieving state-of-the-art performance on visual recognition tasks. Some digital retinas are designed to be highly efficient and require minimal computational resources, while others are designed to be highly accurate and can achieve state-of-the-art performance.

The First Part of the Multimedia Turing Test

The purpose of this research is to provide a definition of "multimedia intelligence" as well as a description of the interactive feedback loop that exists between AI and multimedia. Fig. (**1**). Recent research has concentrated on bridging the gap between AI (machine learning) and multimedia, but research going in the opposite direction, from AI (machine learning) to multimedia, has lagged substantially behind. We believe that a multimedia version of the Turing test would be an effective way to complete the loop. In a multimedia Turing test, the Turing test is carried out on a number of different multimedia modalities, including visual (visual and text), audio (audio and tcxt), *etc*. modalities. In this part of the article, we examine the visual Turing test and argue that the other parts of the multimedia Turing test will adhere to the same pattern. In order to take the next step toward creating more human-like thinking for multimedia, a computer algorithm may need to pass the visual Turing test. This test attempts to determine whether or not a computer is capable of acquiring concepts on the same level as humans. The visual Turing test was developed because of humans' innate ability to comprehend visual information and generate narratives, which motivated the exam's creation. A visual Turing test attempts to simulate the way in which people look at pictures by presenting both the test machine and the human with an image and a sequence of questions that are organised to follow the natural progression of a story. If we ask people a series of questions about an image and check if they can properly identify the object in the picture, we can use the visual Turing test to determine whether or not they can differentiate between a computer and a human.

However, humans are unable to make this determination. It is abundantly clear that a reasoning capacity comparable to that of a human is necessary in order to pass the visual Turing test. The improvement of thinking processes that are applicable to multimedia is an interesting and potentially fruitful topic for further research. For instance, we can readily enrich deep neural networks with reasoning characteristics by incorporating a variety of reasoning traits into the networks themselves. DNNs could have their representation capacity increased by adding additional and better reasoning-augmented layers or modules to the architecture. GNNs can be used to both link together multimedia artefacts in heterogeneous networks and to depict the connections between these networks. In this case, it will be fruitful to combine the relational reasoning capability of GNN with human-like multi-step reasoning in order to develop a new GNN framework with an increased capacity for reasoning. Looking at it from a more in-depth perspective, the most appealing aspect of human-like cognitive learning (perception-reasoning cascade learning in Fig. (**5**) is that the reasoning process is visible and explainable, so we know how and why our models will act towards a specific scenario. This makes human-like cognitive learning one of the most promising areas of research in the field of artificial intelligence. Because of this, it is worthwhile to investigate the prospect of constructing more robust reasoning models by making use of first-order logic, a logic programming language, or even a domain-specific language in conjunction with a more flexible reasoning approach. An additional promising route toward explainable reasoning in multimedia is the automation of program language designing and programmer executors. This will make it possible to use neural-symbolic reasoning in more complex contexts, which is an important step toward explainable reasoning in the field. The integration of neural networks and reasoning through a framework that allows for joint optimization is essential to the realisation of the vision of explainable reasoning in multimedia. This is because, at the moment, the neural networks and the reasoning modules are optimised in a manner that is independent of one another.

META-LEARNING AND AUTOMATIC MACHINE LEARNING

Meta-learning and Automatic Machine Learning (AutoML) are similar but distinct ideas that both focus on improving the efficacy and efficiency of machine learning. Meta-learning is defined as the process of learning how to learn. Meta-learning, often known as "learning to learn," is a method of training machine learning models that enables them to adapt quickly to new tasks or situations. It is a form of training that is used in artificial intelligence. A meta-learning model is one that is trained on a wide variety of tasks so that it can learn to recognise patterns or features that are prevalent across a variety of activities. A model that has not been meta-trained cannot compete with its ability to learn new tasks more rapidly and with fewer data points than it can. On the other side, AutoML is a technique for automatically constructing, training, and optimising machine learning models. It is a form of automation. It makes use of algorithms to search through a wide space including a variety of alternative models, hyperparameters, and architectures in order to locate the most suitable one for a specific undertaking. Data scientists, who often spend a large amount of time on this procedure, could benefit from this as they could save time and costs.

Both meta-learning and automatic machine learning (AutoML) are currently active areas of research that have been demonstrated to be effective in a variety of different applications. They are complementary tools that can be utilised jointly to enhance the capabilities of machine learning models. For instance, a meta-learned model may be applied as an initialization to an AutoML algorithm, which would enable the system to converge on the best solution in a shorter amount of time.

Meta-learning and Automatic Machine Learning (AutoML) are two interesting concepts that have the potential to improve the overall performance of AI models when applied to multimedia tasks. The application of meta-learning to multimedia tasks can be accomplished by training a model on a wide variety of multimedia datasets, including still photos, moving images, audio files, and video files. Because of this, the model is able to learn to recognise similar patterns and features across many types of multimedia, which can help it adapt to new multimedia jobs in a more timely and effective manner. On the other side, AutoML is a tool that may be used to automate the process of constructing machine learning models and refining them for use in multimedia activities. For instance, an AutoML algorithm could be used to search through a large space of possible model architectures and hyperparameters in order to find the optimal one for a particular multimedia task, such as image classification or video analysis. This would allow the algorithm to find the optimal model architecture for the task. When applied to multimedia work, the combination of meta-learning and AutoML can have a significant impact. For instance, a meta-learned model may be applied as an initialization to an AutoML algorithm, which would enable the system to converge on the best solution in a shorter amount of time. In addition, the meta-learned model can direct the search that the AutoML algorithm performs, assisting the system in concentrating its efforts on the most fruitful regions of the search space. Overall, Meta-learning and AutoML are key concepts for performing multimedia activities with AI, and they are actively being investigated in the field. This can assist in improving the performance of AI models and make them more accessible to users who have less knowledge of the subject.

Fig. (7) illustrates the concept of visual question answering (VQA) using DF (Deep Features). VQA refers to automatically answering questions about an image or graphic content. In this context, DF likely refers to deep learning-based features extracted from the visual data.

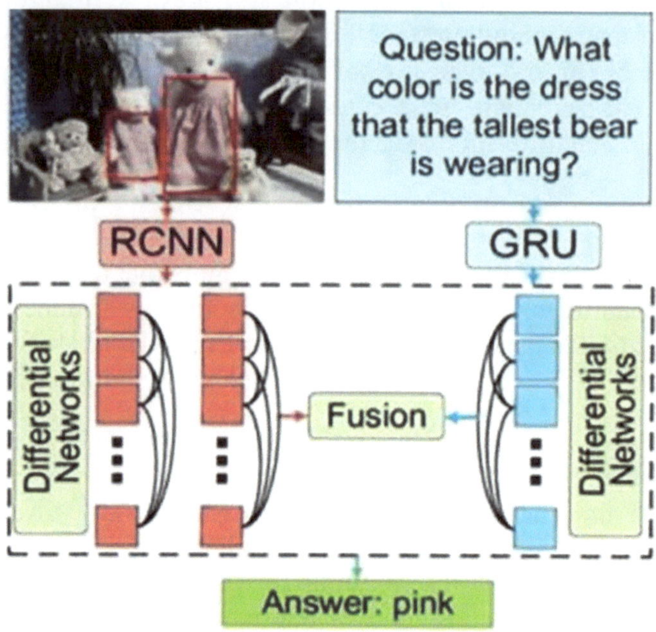

Fig. (7). Visual question answering using DF.

The figure suggests that DF, obtained from deep learning models, can be utilized to enhance the performance of VQA systems. These deep features capture meaningful representations of visual content and can be used to understand and interpret images more effectively. By incorporating DF into the VQA framework, the system can extract relevant information from images and provide accurate answers to questions asked about them.

The integration of DF with VQA systems can improve the system's ability to comprehend visual content, enabling it to answer a wide range of questions related to the images. This approach leverages the power of deep learning and image understanding to facilitate more advanced and accurate visual question answering.

Overall, Fig. (7) highlights the application of DF in visual question answering and emphasizes the potential for improving the performance of VQA systems by incorporating deep features extracted from images using deep learning techniques.

CONCLUSION

In this study, we discuss the confluence of AI and multimedia in the era of "big data." We offer the innovative idea of Multimedia Intelligence, which investigates the interaction between multimedia and artificial intelligence. The investigation involves the two following directions:

1) Multimedia increases the explicability of AI.

2) Artificial intelligence makes multimedia more inferable.

Multimedia inputs, such as images, videos, and audio, can increase the explicability of AI in several ways. Firstly, multimedia inputs often provide more context and information than text inputs alone, making it easier for humans to understand the reasoning behind an AI model's decisions. For example, an AI model that is trained on images of animals can provide its reasoning for identifying an animal as a specific species by showing an image of the animal in question. This can help to increase trust in the model and its decisions. Secondly, multimedia inputs are often more intuitive and accessible to non-experts, making it easier for them to understand the AI model and its functioning. For example, a video of a self-driving car can demonstrate its decision-making process in a way that is easy to understand, even for those with no technical background. Additionally, multimedia inputs can also be used to create interactive visualizations that allow users to explore the AI model's decision-making process and understand how it arrived at a particular decision. Lastly, Multimedia inputs can also be used to generate explanations through text, audio, or even videos, this can further help to increase the explicability of the AI model. Overall, the use of multimedia inputs can help to increase the explicability of AI, making it easier for humans to understand and trust the decisions made by the model.

Artificial intelligence (AI) can make multimedia more inferable in several ways.

Firstly, AI can be used to analyze and extract insights from multimedia data, such as images, videos, and audio. For example, an AI-powered image recognition model can identify objects, people, and other features in an image, making it easier for humans to understand the content of the image. Similarly, an AI-powered speech recognition model can transcribe audio into text, making it easier for humans to understand the content of audio files. Secondly, AI can be used to generate new multimedia content that is based on existing multimedia data. For example, an AI-powered text-to-speech model can generate an audio file from text, making it easier for humans to understand the content of text-based documents. Similarly, an AI-powered image generation model can generate new images from existing images, making it easier for humans to understand the content of images. Thirdly, AI can be used to create interactive multimedia experiences that allow users to explore and understand multimedia data in new ways. For example, an AI-powered virtual reality model can create immersive experiences that allow users to explore and understand complex data in a more intuitive way. Lastly, AI can be used to generate explanations or summaries of multimedia data, making it easier for humans to understand the main idea or insights contained within the data.

Overall, AI can make multimedia more inferable by providing insights, generating new multimedia, creating interactive experiences and providing explanations, which can help humans to better understand and process the information contained within multimedia data.

REFERENCES

[1] Z. Wenwu, W. Xin, and G. Wen, "Multimedia intelligence: When multimedia meets artificial intelligence", *IEEE Transactions on Multimedia* vol. 22, no. 7, pp. 1823-1835, 2020.

[2] A. George, "Intelligent interactive multimedia systems and services in practice", 2015. [http://dx.doi.org/10.1007/978-3-319-17744-1]

[3] X. Wang, and W. Zhu, "Guohao li perceptual visual reasoning with knowledge propagation", *Conference: the 27th ACM International Conference,* October 2019, pp 530–538 . [http://dx.doi.org/10.1145/3343031.3350922]

[4] W.L.J.X.W.R.L. Chenfei, "Differential Networks for Visual Question Answering", *Proceedings of the AAAI Conference on Artificial Intelligence 33,* vol. 33, no. 01, pp. 8997-9004, 2019. [http://dx.doi.org/10.1609/aaai.v33i01.33018997]

[5] C. Wu, J. Liu, and X. Wang, "Differential networks for visual question answering", *Proceedings of the AAAI Conference on Artificial Intelligence,,* vol. 33, no. 01, pp. 8997-9004, 2019.

[6] P. Anderson, X. He, C. Buehler, D. Teney, M. Johnson, S. Gould, and L. Zhang, "Bottom-up and top-down attention for image captioning and visual question answering", *2018 IEEE/CVF Conference on Computer Vision and Pattern Recognition,* 18-23 June 2018, Salt Lake City, UT, USA, pp. 6077-6086, [http://dx.doi.org/10.1109/CVPR.2018.00636]

[7] J. Andreas, M. Rohrbach, T. Darrell, and D. Klein, "Neural module networks", *2016 IEEE Conference on Computer Vision and Pattern Recognition (CVPR)* 27-30 June 2016, Las Vegas, NV, USA, pp. 39-48.
[http://dx.doi.org/10.1109/CVPR.2016.12]

[8] S. Antol, A. Agrawal, J. Lu, M. Mitchell, D. Batra, C. Lawrence Zitnick, and D. Parikh, "Vqa: Visual question answering. In ICCV", In: *Proceedings of the IEEE International Conference on Computer Vision*, 2015, pp. 2425-2433.

[9] H. Ben-younes, R. Cadene, M. Cord, and N. Thome, "MUTAN: Multimodal tucker fusion for visual question answering", *arXiv:1705.06676,* pp. 2631-2639.

[10] K. Chen, J. Wang, L-C. Chen, H. Gao, W. Xu, and R. Nevatia, "ABC-CNN: An attention based convolutional neural network for visual question answering", *arXiv:1511.05960,* .

[11] K. Cho, B. van Merrienboer, D. Bahdanau, and Y Bengio, "On the properties of neural machine translation: Encoderdecoder approaches", *arXiv:1409.1259.* [http://dx.doi.org/10.3115/v1/W14-4012]

[12] A. Fukui, D.H. Park, D. Yang, A. Rohrbach, T. Darrell, and M. Rohrbach, Multimodal compact

bilinear pooling for visual question answering and visual grounding. *Proceedings of the 2016 Conference on Empirical Methods in Natural Language Processing* Association for Computational Linguistics, 2016, pp. 457-468.
[http://dx.doi.org/10.18653/v1/D16-1044]

[13] M. Gonen, and E. Alpaydın, "Multiple kernel learning algorithms", *J. Mach. Learn. Res.,* vol. 12, no. Jul, pp. 2211-2268, 2011.

[14] Z. Ghahramani, and M.I. Jordan, "Factorial hidden markov models", *Adv. Neural Inf. Process. Syst.,* pp. 472-478, 1996.

[15] V. Nefian, L. Liang, X. Pi, L. Xiaoxiang, C. Mao, and K. Murphy, "A coupled hmm for audio-visual speech recognition", *2002 IEEE International Conference on Acoustics, Speech, and Signal Processing* 05-09 June 2000, Istanbul, Turkey, pp. 0-1.

[16] J. Lafferty, A. McCallum, and F. C. Pereira, "Conditional random fields: Probabilistic models for segmenting and labeling sequence data", *Proceedings of the Eighteenth International Conference on Machine Learning* 28 June 2001, pp.282–289.

[17] J. Ngiam, A. Khosla, M. Kim, J. Nam, H. Lee, and A.Y. Ng, "Multimodal deep learning", *Proceedings of the 28th international conference on machine learning (ICML-11)* pp.689-696, year.2011.

[18] S. Hochreiter, and J. Schmidhuber, "Long short-term memory", *Neural Comput.,* vol. 9, no. 8, pp. 1735-1780, 1997.
[http://dx.doi.org/10.1162/neco.1997.9.8.1735] [PMID: 9377276]

[19] M. Wöllmer, M. Kaiser, F. Eyben, B. Schuller, and G. Rigoll, "LSTM-Modeling of continuous emotions in an audiovisual affect recognition framework", *Image Vis. Comput.,* vol. 31, no. 2, pp. 153-163, 2013.
[http://dx.doi.org/10.1016/j.imavis.2012.03.001]

[20] X. Wang, W. Zhu, and C. Liu, "Semi-supervised deep quantization for cross-modal search", *Proceedings of the 27th ACM International Conference on Multimedia* October 2019, pp.1730-1739. year.2019.
[http://dx.doi.org/10.1145/3343031.3350934]

[21] T. Mikolov, I. Sutskever, K. Chen, G.S. Corrado, and J. Dean, "Distributed representations of words and phrases and their compositionality", *Adv. Neural Inf. Process. Syst.,* pp. 3111-3119, 2013.

[22] M. Baroni, "Grounding distributional semantics in the visual world", *Lang. Linguist. Compass,* vol. 10, no. 1, pp. 3-13, 2016.
[http://dx.doi.org/10.1111/lnc3.12170]

[23] R. Socher, M. Ganjoo, C.D. Manning, and A. Ng, "Zero-shot learning through cross-modal transfer", *Adv. Neural Inf. Process. Syst.,* pp. 935-943, 2013.

[24] J. Rajendran, M.M. Khapra, S. Chandar, and B Ravindran, "Bridge correlational neural networks for multilingual multimodal representation learning", *arXiv:1510.03519.*

[25] P. Nakov, and H.T. Ng, "Improving statistical machine translation for a resource-poor language using related resource-rich languages", *J. Artif. Intell. Res.,* vol. 44, pp. 179-222, 2012.
[http://dx.doi.org/10.1613/jair.3540]

SUBJECT INDEX

A

B

C

Suman Kumar Swarnkar, Sapna Singh Kshatri, Virendra Kumar Swarnkar & Tien Anh Tran (Eds.)

D

E

F

G

H

I

K

L

M

N

P

R

S

T

V

W

www.ingramcontent.com/pod-product-compliance
Lightning Source LLC
LaVergne TN
LVHW070126110826
845147LV00002B/192

* 9 7 8 9 8 1 5 1 9 6 4 6 7 *